# Breaking Down The Walls of New Jericho

# ELKAN V. KEMP

## Breaking Down The Walls of New Jericho

Those questions you asked as a child but were shushed.
As an adult you quit asking.

**Markas Publishing**

# DEDICATION

I would like to personally dedicate this book to my loving wife, Nettie E. Kemp, who has been a true help to me for more than 50 years and whose devotion has made all my work possible. This book is also dedicated to our three sons who, like their mother, were deprived of much of my attention while they were growing up because Uncle Sam and others made such strong demands upon my time.

I gratefully acknowledged that, without the steadfastness and devotion of Jews (in spite of ages of persecution), there would be no Bible and no Judaeo-Christian religion.

*Reverend Elkan V. Kemp*

Front Cover Design: Robert Tourt

Library of Congress Cataloging-in-Publication Data 94-075674

ISBN: 1-878455-09-5

Published By: Markas Publishing, P.O.Box 415, Dublin, OH 43017

Copyright ©1994, Elkan Vern Kemp

All rights reserved. No part of this book may be reproduced or transmitted in any form or by any means, electronic or mechanical, including photocopying, recording, or any information storage and retrieval system, without permission in writing from the author.

Printed in the United States of America

# INTRODUCTION

This book of essays is an attempt to present, in concise form, subjects that will focus on religious ideas troublesome to many thinking seekers of the true God. Each essay is meant to carry one through a subject without requiring considerable research on neighboring ideas. It is a sincere attempt to encourage serious people to delve deeply into their beliefs and convictions—to think carefully, joyously and productively about the God they worship.

I find this particularly urgent due to the number of people I have found trying to do this as they approach their last moments in this life. That is not an appropriate time to do so. There are too many calls upon our love at that time. Witness the accounts of Jesus on the Cross.

I depend heavily upon the Bible in the original languages as applied to daily living and upon the multitude of good questions raised by many devoted Bible students during my more than 50 years as a teacher. My goal is that together we may arrive at a good common sense which I perceive to be inspiration. Of course, inspiration of this kind comes only to those sincerely wanting a practical or useful knowledge of the only true God.

I hope by this means to stir up the minds of those who care about morality, social obligations and relationships with all of YAHWEH'S creatures and His creation in general. When each person becomes the sole source and reason for his values—when morality is only relative— making each one his own god, the whole of humanity becomes unzipped and pours forth the bedlam seen in our world of the 30's and on through the 80's.

Only one true God, YAHWEH the Creator, can give order and

stability to life on earth. Our congress of some years ago was spiritually moved to add "under God" to our pledge to the flag. But to find this true God requires the full devotion of mind and being. It requires an absolute devotion to the truth no matter what the consequences to our strongest convictions—even church or synagogue dogmas and doctrines. For some, this may lead to painful psycho-surgery. But, it will be found to be worth it. This kind of labor is what I would call true prayer. Out of it wholesome answers will come. The fruits of such labor would be multiplied many fold if several people gather in a family or a group of friends for sharing in study and discussion.

These essays are planned as a primer to challenge deep thought and so to stimulate discovery. Each essay can give sufficient stimulus for a single sitting or meeting except for those titled IMAGE OF GOD and THE GOLDEN THREAD. These two essays may require several meetings or sittings to cover the material therein. By the grace of YAHWEH, some may even be led to careful, serious reading of the Bible—regularly.

For these reasons, the essays of this book are not meant to be read quickly or lightly. It will take careful thought and self-examination to reap the inner peace and sense of direction that I covet for each of my brothers and sisters in the Kingdom of God. I have tried to keep each essay as short as possible so that one may give less time to reading and more to thinking or listening to the Father speak as a means to rewarding spiritual growth. May you be blessed with the questions that come from a hunger to know the truth. I would also covet for you the stability of religious thought that comes from a growing familiarity with the <u>whole</u> Bible.

The use of Hebrew, Aramaic and Greek words in the text is only meant to supply more advance scholars with the bases of my translations. Those not acquainted with these languages may simply read past them without loss.

One more thing for your attention: some may feel at times that I am preaching. I suppose I am, because I feel so strongly on some of my beliefs. But these are <u>my</u> beliefs. I do not expect them to be yours unless they fit with your experiences of God.

# PREFACE

## Some Questions Giving Rise To These Chapters

(Please use them as a warm-up on each subject)

### PART 1 - ABOUT THE BIBLE

Chapter 1 - On Scripture in General
1. With all the fervent attempts to destroy the Bible and the people of the Bible, why is it still the best known and available book in the world?
2. Why is it so full of wrath, vengeance and violence?
3. How can we rely on a book so full of contradictions?
4. Why is it that so many are driven apart by the different interpretations of the Bible?

Chapter 2 - About Bible Translations
1. Why are there so many different translations of the Bible?
2. How can we know which is right or true?
3. Is there any hope that we can ever know what was orignally said or written?
4. Why bother if it is so difficult?

Chapter 3 - . . . Genocide in the Bible
    1. Why?
    2. Is this to say it is right?
    3. How did the people of the Old Testament manage to survive?
    4. Are we above such atrocities today?

Chapter 4 - . . . On the Use of the Pronoun He
    1. Why is God always referred to as "he" in the Bible?
    2. Why not use some other pronoun in respect of female humans?

Chapter 5 - . . . The Sacred name
    1. In the light of Exodus 3:14f., why is the use of the name YAHWEH avoided by so many?
    2. It sounds so strange, why use it at all?

## PART 2 - ABOUT THE CHURCH

Chapter 6 - Creeds . . .
    1. What is meant by a "creed"?
    2. Why do we have creeds when they divide the people of YAHWEH so severely?
    3. What is the danger of creeds—why do they divide us?
    4. What then, should we do about them?
    5. Did Jesus of Nazareth establish any creeds?

Chapter 7 - . . . Habit in Human Nature
    1. Are habits good or bad?
    2. If bad, how shall we get rid of them?
    3. If useful, how shall we keep them good?
    4. What about habit in religious rituals?

Chapter 8 - Of Priests and Clergy
    1. How did priests become a part of religion?
    2. Why are they made so important in the Bible?
    3. What is their effect upon the Judaeo-Christian religion?
    4. Is there a place for priests in modern religious practices?

## PART 3 - RELIGIOUS COMMUNICATION

Chapter 9 - On Prophecy and the "Word"
    1. What is meant by "the word of YAHWEH"?
    2. How can we know when we hear it?
    3. What is the meaning of the word "prophet"?
    4. Then, what is prophecy?
    5. How is this applied to "truth" in the Bible?

Chapter 10 - Ways YAHWEH Speaks
    1. We say God is spirit. How, then, can He speak without a mouth?
    2. If we say He speaks through the Bible, how can we sort out what He is saying in the different translations and interpretations?
    3. What are some of the other ways YAHWEH speaks to us as individuals?
    4. Does He also speak to nations? How?

Chapter 11 - Communication-Prayer...
    1. Is there a special physical attitude for prayer taught in the Bible?
    2. If, as Psalm 139 says, YAHWEH knows every thought before we can put it into words, what place is there for prayer?
    3. If He knows all our needs as well as our wants, what about the Psalms and forms of church prayer?
    4. Didn't Jesus teach his disciples the "Lord's Prayer"?
    5. Well, what about that "prayer"? How shall we pray?

6. What about religious incantations?
   7. What about "speaking in tongues"?

Chapter 12 - Passing On the True Religion
   1. We have the Bible accessible to most people of the world, what more do we need to perpetuate the Judaeo-Christian religion?
   2. With the break-up of the family in much of the world, how is the true religion to be passed on?
   3. What is to be done to correct this?


## PART 4 - THE NATURE OF GOD

Chapter 13 - On the Creator and His Creation
   1. Who made God?
   2. What did God use to make the universe?
   3. How does science fit in here?
   4. Since God created all that is, why did He create Humans (such as they are)?
   5. How do we know all this?

Chapter 14 - The Image of God
   1. What does it mean to say that humans are made in the image of God?
   2. If YAHWEH is infinite spirit, how can we be like Him? We are physical, aren't we?
   3. What characteristics do humans have in common with our Creator?
   4. So we are both persons. How then can we communicate with One who has no mouth to speak or ears to hear? (You may need to return to the essay on communication, Part 3)
   5. How can we be free if we are created to be the way we are?

Chapter 15 - The Presence of God
   1. How can we know YAHWEH'S presence in us? What does that mean?
   2. I am not used to thinking like this. How can I understand it?

Chapter 16 - Spirit...
   1. How do we come to use the word "spirit" for God?
   2. Since this idea is so abstract, how can we even speak of Him?
   3. How can we begin to know Him?

## PART 5 - SIN AND ATONEMENT

Chapter 17 - What Is Sin?
   1. What is it?
   2. Are the Old Testament ideas different from those of the New Testament? How?

Chapter 18 - Forgiveness-Atonement
   1. What led to sacrifice as a means of achieving forgiveness?
   2. Thinking of sin as defined in chapter 17, how can sacrifice bring about atonement? Why?
   3. With the teachings of the "ethical prophets" and Ezekiel and Psalm 50, how could one believe in ritual sacrifice as a means to atonement?
   4. What then, is the means to YAHWEH'S forgiveness? Why?
   5. What then, is the unforgivable (mortal) sin?

Chapter 19 - ...Substitutionary Atonement
   1. What is meant by this?
   2. How can a price be paid and forgiveness still be free grace?
   3. What would be the true virtue in Jesus' life if he was made

virtuous?
4. If he was so different, as tradition makes him, how can we be like him?
5. But why did Jesus have to choose death on the Cross?

Chapter 20 - Satan...
1. Why is Satan so infrequently mentioned in the Old Testament?
2. Where did the idea come from?
3. If we are responsible for our sin, how can we put the blame on Satan or anyone else?
4. What is the proper place for this character in the Judaeo-Christian religion?

## PART 6 - LIFE, DEATH AND AFTER

Chapter 21 - "Life" and "Death" in the Bible
1. Do these words have the same meaning in both the Old and New Testaments?
2. How are they viewed in each Testament? How do they each compare with our own views?
3. Why are there such differences? What similarities do we find?
4. What do the gospels say that Jesus taught about life and death?

Chapter 22 - "Salvation"
1. What does this word mean to us as individuals?
2. How was it used in the Old and New Testaments?
3. What specifically was Jesus' view of "salvation"?
4. How do we find or achieve it?
5. Is it available to all or just to a few? How do we know?

Chapter 23 - Heaven and Hell?
1. If there is no life after death, where is the justice in YAHWEH'S creation?

2. What did the poet who gave us the book of Job say? How is this different from the rest of the Old Testament?
3. Why are such ideas as heaven and hell necessary anyway?
4. What does this have to do with "freedom of choice" and "love"?
5. Are heaven and hell physical states of being?

## PART 7 - SON OF GOD, MESSIAH

Chapter 24 - "Son of God" in the Bible
1. How does the Bible use this expression? Old Testament? New Testament?
2. What are the main differences? Why?
3. What was the title that Jesus used of himself most frequently?
4. How does he respond when he is asked if he is "the Son of God"?

Chapter 25 - Messiah...
1. How does the use of this word in the Old Testament compare with its use in the New Testament?
2. Who was the first king anointed in the New Testament sense of Messiah, Lord and Savior?
3. Was this role limited to Jews?
4. Was Jesus ever so anointed? Who anointed him?

Chapter 26 - On the "Second Coming"
1. What do Christians mean by this expression?
2. How can it be since our bodies die?
3. When did Jesus say he would come with the Kingdom of God?
4. What one historical event fulfilled Jesus' Promise of his coming with the Kingdom of God?

Chapter 27 - King of Kings...
1. When was this title first used in the Bible? Of whom?

2. How and why did Israel make for themselves a king?
3. How did YAHWEH take it?
4. By whom was it applied to Jesus? Could he have accepted it?

## PART 8 - ON THE PHYSICAL RESURRECTION

Chapter 28 - ...The Dogma of the Physical Resurrection
1. What are the first accounts in the Bible of persons taken to be with God?
2. What about the story of Samuel being called up by a medium?
3. Who are the first to be considered resurrected in the New Testament?
4. What did Jesus say about physical resurrection?
5. How did Paul view life after death of the body?

Chapter 29 - On the Book of Job
1. What did this poet have to say about life after death of the body?
2. What other values do you find in this book?
3. How is it structured?
4. This poem is protest literature. What is it protesting?
5. What part does the prose beginning and ending play?

Chapter 30 - Who wrote the Gospel of John? ... What does this gospel say about the resurrection of Jesus?
1. How did this gospel come to be attributed to the Apostle?
2. Did the same writer write all the books attributed to him?
3. How can we ever know who actually wrote this gospel?
4. What does it say about Jesus' resurrection?

## PART 9 - MATURE RELIGION

Chapter 31 - The Golden Thread

1. What is meant by this expression?
2. Has there been a steady progression of religious understanding among individual humans? Why or why not?
3. Does the Bible present an orderly progression from ignorance to religious maturity?
4. How did this understanding grow? (How has it grown?)

Chapter 32 - Anything Less Is Idolatry
1. How do you understand the word "idolatry"?
2. What does the Bible mean by it?
3. Are there signs of it in our world today?
4. How can we tell idolatry from worship of the true God?

## PART 10 - PUTTING IT ALL TOGETHER

Chapter 33 - Mystery
1. What do you mean by the word "mystery"?
2. What do you think of Deuteronomy 29:29 as a definition?
3. Does it define it for you satisfactorily?
4. What are some real mysteries as you see them? (Spirit, thought, mind, infinity?)
5. Why is mystery a mystery to us? How real is it?

Chapter 34 - Heaven Here and Now
1. Where are heaven and hell? When?
2. How do we attain either?
3. How may we stay in heaven?

Chapter 35 - I Believe Because
1. What do you mean by "believe"? (Have faith in?)
2. How and why do you believe?
3. How can one believe in YAHWEH—an infinite spirit?
4. What do you believe and why?
5. Who is your God and why?

# Table of Contents

Introduction ..................................................................................................i
Preface: Some Questions Giving Rise To These Chapters ......................iii

**PART 1: ABOUT THE BIBLE** ..................................................................1

Chapter 1:  On Scripture In General ........................................................3
Chapter 2:  About Bible Translations ......................................................5
Chapter 3:  About Those Horrible Acts of Genocide in the Bible ...............9
Chapter 4:  Male and Female, on the Use of the Pronoun "He" ..............13
Chapter 5:  YAHWEH, The Sacred Name ..............................................17

**PART 2: ABOUT THE CHURCH** ..........................................................21

Chapter 6:  Creeds and Fragmentation of the Church and Synagogue .......23
Chapter 7:  Ritual to Rote to Paganism--Habit in Human Nature ............27
Chapter 8:  Of Priests and Clergy ..........................................................31

**PART 3: ON RELIGIOUS COMMUNICATION** ......................................35

Chapter 9: On Prophecy and the "Word" ................................................. 37
Chapter 10: Ways YAHWEH Speaks ................................................. 41
Chapter 11: Communication--Prayer--Incantations--"Tongues" ................. 47
Chapter 12: Passing on the True Religion ................................................. 55

## PART 4: THE NATURE OF GOD ................................................. 59

Chapter 13: On the Creator and Creation ................................................. 61
Chapter 14: The Image of God ................................................. 65
Chapter 15: The Presence of God ................................................. 73
Chapter 16: Spirit--What It Is, What It Does, How It Is Known ................. 77

## PART 5: SIN AND ATONEMENT ................................................. 81

Chapter 17: What Is Sin? ................................................. 83
Chapter 18: Forgiveness--Atonement ................................................. 85
Chapter 19: The Dogma of Substitutionary Atonement ............................. 89
Chapter 20: Satan, That Old Devil, the Serpent ........................................ 93

## PART 6: LIFE, DEATH AND AFTER ................................................. 97

Chapter 21: Life and Death in the Bible ................................................. 99
Chapter 22: "Salvation" in the Bible ................................................. 105
Chapter 23: Heaven and Hell ................................................. 111

## PART 7: SON OF GOD, MESSIAH ................................................. 117

Chapter 24: "Son of God" in the Bible ................................................. 119
Chapter 25: Messiah-Christos-Anointed ................................................. 123
Chapter 26: On the Second Coming ("Adventism") ............................... 127
Chapter 27: King of Kings and Lord of Lords and Subjects ..................... 131

## PART 8: ON THE PHYSICAL RESURRECTION ............................... 135

Chapter 28:  Some Questions Raised By the Dogma
               of the Physical Reurrection .................................................... 137
Chapter 29:  On the Book of Job  (The Old Testament) .............................. 143
Chapter 30:  Who Wrote the Gospel of John? ............................................. 147

# PART 9:  MATURE RELIGION ................................................................ 153

Chapter 31:  The Golden Thread ................................................................ 155
Chapter 32:  Anything Less Is Idolatry ...................................................... 163

# PART 10:  PUTTING IT ALL TOGETHER ............................................... 169

Chapter 33:  Mystery .................................................................................. 171
Chapter 34:  Heaven Here and Now ........................................................... 175
Chapter 35:  I Believe Because ................................................................... 179

# INDEX ........................................................................................................ 185

# PART 1

## ABOUT THE BIBLE

# Chapter 1

# On Scripture In General

There have been innumerable attempts to destroy, nullify, adulterate or simply reject some or all of the books that make up the "Holy Bible". The very fact that it has survived at all must be considered miraculous. Its influence is felt in every culture and every religion of mankind except for the most isolated and primitive of peoples who have never been contacted by humans from outside their society. Even these are governed by rules in their culture that embody generally the essence of the last six of the Ten Commandments. Obviously, these commandments fit all of humanity—naturally.

Just as children up to the age of three are steeped in a "No"' environment and so (sometimes called the terrible two's) at times appear to have a one word vocabulary "No!" so also the primitive rules of the earliest religions are put negatively. It is not difficult to see therefore, why most of the Bible uses a negative approach to teaching. This includes the lessons of history there-in.

The Creator had the same problems with His human creatures that parents have with very young children. Those things permitted, do little to stimulate curiosity—one of the strongest urges in the human psyche. The moment anything is prohibited curiosity is aroused in one, and from that moment on the person is driven by the question, "Why?" The divine origin of the truth in the story of Adam and Eve in the Garden of Eden (Genesis 3:1ff.) is obvious. How universal is the response! Humans have not changed noticeably from our earliest knowledge of them. "... Did God say, 'You shall not eat of any tree of the garden?' and the woman said...'We may eat of the fruit of the trees of the garden.' But God said, "You shall not eat of the fruit of the tree which is in the midst of the garden..."'" Of all the trees available to them, which one did they go after? Naturally, the one prohibited—the one "in the midst of the garden". Why does one never think to touch test paint on a wall unless there is a sign saying "Wet Paint"? So it is that the "Holy Bible" is full of truth mostly registered in negative form.

It is to be expected that, since the Bible contains all that mankind has ever thought about God and man and the relationship between them as well as man's relationship to man, the truth it expresses is often the wrong way humans have thought. It is this fact that confuses any who make a half-hearted attempt at reading the Bible. Probably of no other subject than the Bible is it more true to say, "A little knowledge is a dangerous thing."

Not only is it true of Christianity, but also of Hebrew and Muslim religious seekers, that divisions among them spring directly from ignorance, misuse, and abuse of the Bible. There might be still some disagreement over the politics of their congregations, but dogma and doctrine would be produced from unity rather than from violent disagreement over what the Bible says, if they knew it well.

Religious peace can come among us only if we will take the whole book as it is instead of taking it in parts bent to fit our peculiar prejudices. It is clear that, if the Creator had sat and dictated the entire Bible to faithful, infallible scribes who wrote and preserved it intact to this very day—there would be absolutely no contradictions, twice told tales different from each other, fragmented language with parts omitted or words lost. What we have in the best, most literal translations and in the original Hebrew, Aramaic and Greek is adequate for learning all that is good and true as well as what is not true or "bad". It is, in spite of its fallible editors, adequate for knowing all that is true of the nature of God, of man, of the relationship between them and of the proper relationship between humans on earth. I gather, from the state of humanity and our world in the twentieth century, that this is truth worth knowing.

# Chapter 2

## About Bible Translations

Every culture develops around and in a particular environment. People who come out of similar environments naturally find it easier to understand each other. Communication between them, therefore, is not difficult. On the other hand, contrasting backgrounds of experience make communication a difficult problem even if they speak the same language. This may explain why marriages between persons of radically different cultures are frequently stormy and, at times, downright destructive. Is it any wonder then that nations, likewise of contrasting backgrounds, are suspicious, insensitive to each other and often violent in their behavior toward each other?

When it comes to religion (the core of motivation, goals and ideals of a person) compatibility can be vital to peaceful relationships between persons. Each religion has its own language. Just try to understand the ideas of a Buddhist, Muslim, Shintoist, Christian liberal or Christian literalist or a Christian fundamentalist group of which you are not a part. Add to that the translation of any language into another and problems compound.

If we learn a language as our second language, we shall always possess prejudices built into our own thoughts by our experience, beliefs, and environment. It is extremely difficult for a translator to be completely objective. To be so, one has to steep one's self in the culture of the people from which the language he is translating comes.

## About The Bible

To translate the Bible into English is especially difficult. Modern lexicographers do not base their English dictionary definitions on old meanings in order to establish some stability to the language. Rather, they seek out modern idioms for the meanings of the words they record. This makes the English language so fluid that one can accurately say that we live in a state of Babel. True communication would mean that a word I use carries the same thought to your mind that is represented by that word in mine.

Dead languages such as classical Hebrew, Greek and Latin give us thoughts at a time and place where they originated. Of course, all languages move to some degree. But, in translating the Bible, it is possible (if one cares enough) to study the periods and environments of the various books of which it is made. Thus one may catch the meaning of a word at a point in time in which it is used. Archeology has helped tremendously in that. Also, there are nomadic peoples of the region who still live closely to the old ways of the time of Abraham.

The transition from pastoral-nomadic to agricultural-urban accounts for changes even in classical Hebrew. Add to this the influence of Egypt, Syria, Assyria, Babylon and Phoenicia and you must take great care in translating the Old Testament from the Hebrew and Aramaic into English. It is not impossible, but neither is it easy to know exactly what the translation of a passage ought to be. Then, to put forth a proper English word that bears the same meaning to potential readers as it does to the translator, and you can see the complexity of the problem.

So, what must we do to assure that we receive into our minds accurately what was in the minds of the Bible writers? I would say: "Pray—a lot!" A translator is a teacher and the exhortation of the writer of the epistle of James is quite valid here: "Let not many of you become teachers, my brethren, for you know that we who teach shall be judged with greater strictness." (James 3:1.)

There are helps for us that we may hear truly what the Spirit is saying. E.g., to get the message of Psalm 23, one must crawl inside a sheep and look out through the animal's eyes. Remember, this is not a modern sheep thought of as dumb, flighty and tending to self-destruction and driven by dogs. Old Testament sheep became pets of the shepherd, each given and knowing its name and following in affection out of experience of tender care, firm protection and kindness. One also needs to visualize the barren desert of the Hebrew nomad where an oasis was "Paradise". After scrounging the dry wisps of widely scattered vegetation to find enough to survive, fresh green grass, even enough to lie down in—what a glorious experience! (for a desert sheep of course.) The water in the poem is ideal sheep water—a clear quiet pool. If in this psalm you do not see the loveliest picture that you have ever seen, you have missed its meaning. You see, one must know and feel the background of the writer or, no matter how good the translation, you have missed the message.

The role of the translator of the Bible is a deeply religious one, loaded with the great responsibility that is borne by a prophet. Modern translations that are supposed to make the Bible easier to read can be dangerous. If they are not literal enough for one to feel the grammar and syntax of the original, if they modernize the situation like the Bible subject paintings of the Dark Ages they may well completely mask the true meaning. Study of the Bible is not for lazy people. If a translation is initially easy to read, it is likely miles off the truth of what is being passed on to us by the writers of the Bible.

Remember, for there to be communication, a word has to have the same meaning for all those communicating. Since in our time, few words express the same thought in different minds, we have returned to Babel. The Creator said: "Behold! They are one people and all have one language. Now this is but the beginning of their doings and nothing is being withheld from them that they plan to do." (Genesis 11:6.)

There would be no limit to what we could do if we had one language. Peace and even shalom would be possible. But, we do not have one language and so there is war, ignorance, poverty, crime, diseases, and waste of life and resources in our world. This will continue to be so until we have a single language in which each word means the same to each person. For then it will be possible to unite under the one only true God to pass on that knowledge accurately.

People must study and share together for some time before this can take place between and among them. It takes an intimate acquaintance with each other in order that words become a fair means of communication. Friendly discussion groups of long standing are the best means to this end, especially if the subject matter is one's own religion. Such fellowship can iron out many of the problems related to learning from a Bible written in strange tongues by people who were a part of a society very much different from our own.

# Chapter 3

# About Those Horrible Acts of Genocide in the Bible

In the days when the American Indians lived in a hunting culture, it became necessary from time to time to eliminate competition for game in a particular territory. This was done by competing groups making war on one another. With the human population reduced, the survivors could manage on the limited supply of game left in the territory. So it was with the nomads of the desert in Sinai and Arabia: when grazing land or water was in short supply for a growing human population, one band or tribe would simply eliminate other bands or tribes. Those remaining would then be able to survive on what was available to them. These bands or tribes finding the nomadic-pastoral economy no longer tolerable or adequate for their survival, sought out the benefits of lands with an agricultural economy. Perhaps, at first, it was enough for the nomads to prey upon the people who labored in agriculture like the Midianites in the time of Gideon. (Judges 6:11.) "...Gideon was beating out wheat in the wine press to conceal it from the Midianites."

In due time, it was found to be more productive (for the nomads) to take the land and engage in agriculture themselves. It appears that some found it possible to move in and dwell peaceably among the farmers. For example, Judges 4:11 and 17: "Now Heber had separated from the Kenites, the descendents of Hobab the father-in-law of Moses, and had pitched his tent as far away as the oak of Zaanannim which is near Kadesh." "...for there was peace between Jabin king of Hazor and the house of Heber the Kenite." But more and larger bands invading the land from the desert found that their only possibility was to displace by force those who dwelt in the land. Thus genocide seemed the appropriate method. The writers of the Bible often use the explanation that it was necessary to keep the invaders from being drawn to pagan forms of worship, the religious practices of the peoples being displaced. We humans always seem able to smother conscience by rationalizations.

Of course there were other motives for the practice of genocide by one group against another. Settlers, as they increased occupation of land in America, often practiced it against the American Indian because of attacks against caravans, homes and settlements. And so the saying was, "The only good Indian is a dead one." The Philistines, in the fertile lowlands along the east shore of the Mediterranean, feeling pressure from the invading bands who began spilling down from the highlands, did their best to eliminate the invaders.

In the anarchic period of the "Judges", as wave after wave of nomads came out of the desert to displace people already in the "Holy Land", the Philistines appeared to be able to hold their own and even to subdue the invaders. It was this helpless state of the unorganized nomads that led them to seek unity under a king. "In those days there was no king in Israel; every man did what was right in his own eyes." (Judges 17:6; 18:1; 21:25.) So they came together around the mythological idea of the 12 tribes descended from one man, Jacob or Israel, and demanded a king. "The people...said, 'No! But we will have a king over us that we also may be like all the nations, and that our king may judge us and go out before us and fight our battles.'" (I Samuel 8:19f.)

David was the first of the kings successful enough to practice genocide methodically. "He defeated Moab, and measured them with a line, making them lie down on the ground. Two lines he measured to be put to death, and one full line to be spared..." (II Samuel 8:2.) The invaders that came through Jericho in the 15th century B.C. are said to have utterly "devoted" (hcarem, made a sacrifice to God of) every living or burnable thing in the city. It was the same with Ai and other cities to follow.

*About Those Horribe Acts of Genocide*

    This may have been economically and politically sound. But the world took quite a different view of the morality of such human treatment of other humans in the practices of Hitler's cohorts. Similar practices of the English against the Scottish people did not stir the world so much. Obviously some changes are being made in the human psyche, but not everywhere. Compare the killing fields in Cambodia and the slaughter of Chinese seeking democracy. There are also the atrocious wars in Vietnam, Africa, Afghanistan, and the former Yugoslavia. Things haven't actually changed all that much since the days of the Old Testament.

# Chapter 4

# Male and Female:
# On the Use of the Pronoun "He"

"So God created the man (ha adham) in His image. In the image of God He created him. Male and female He created them." (Genesis 1:27.) There is no favoring distinction between man and woman in this passage. In the next verse, both are blessed. Both are given the responsibility for subduing (cabhash) and dominating (radhah) the rest of the creatures. Literally, the word cabhash means to "tread down". It is used variously of treading down adversaries and of bringing into bondage. The word radhah means basically to "rule over".

The second account, the more primitive one in Genesis 2:24, says that man and woman ar to become "one flesh". In this version of creation, the man (ish) names the woman (ishshah). This is the feminine companion word of the masculine ish. Man's name given him by God is "adham". The giving of a name makes the giver the ruler over the one named. Genesis 1:26; 2:19f. reveals this process in which the human takes dominance over other creatures just as YAHWEH holds dominion over mankind whom He named adham.

In this particular book, it is to be expected that the male will take his dominance over the female in any way he can. But, as the rabbis at Jamnia argued the matter, one said that, since man was made before woman and the woman was made from man, males are properly pre-eminent. On the

*About The Bible*

other side, it was argued that man was made from dust while woman was made from inspired flesh. Thus the argument for male superiority was defeated.

When one looks to the more mature account of creation found in the first chapter of Genesis, there is no need to elevate one over the other. One can look at the various accounts in Old Testament history and easily see that maleness or femaleness is not a factor in leadership (colored as accounts may be by their male authorship.) Consider Rebekah (Genesis 27:5ff.) or Deborah (Judges 4:4ff.) or Jezebel (I Kings 21:5ff.) or Athaliah (II Kings 11:1ff.) as samples of how individuals of the female category were able to dominate their male contemporaries. So it has been throughout human history in some degree or other. We even have that expression, "The woman behind the throne."

The English words "man" and "woman", are much like the Hebrew equivalents, being only a means of distinguishing male from female humans. The Middle English word "wifmann", is made up of two words: "wif" meaning female and "mann" meaning simply human. So it is with ish and ishshah. Some students of the English language see the modern word woman, an original of "womb" plus man. Normal progression in pronunciation leads regularly to the easier "woman" meaning human with a womb.

Here is the primary distinguishing characteristic that sets them apart. Still, the Hebrew root of the feminine ishshah is the third form of the root anash and means soft or delicate. But this is a concept of femininity hardly suitable among primitive societies where the domestic duties of women are very heavy. One should add to that the fact that women must carry, bear and again carry infants in addition to their other labors.

The modern excitement over the use of the pronoun "he" as referring to YAHWEH, and in the use of the concept man (adham), is unfounded. In most contexts, "he" is a neutral word that means generally humankind. The religiously immature wish still to make their god in their own image. Granted, warriors were mainly men in human history. The Old Testament often portrays YAHWEH as a great warrior. This is also evidence of religious immaturity, an anthropomorphism in which YAHWEH is given human characteristics.

## On the Use of the Pronoun "He"

The very meaning of the name YAHWEH, makes such concepts ridiculous. Our temporary confinement to the physical body makes it difficult to escape any tendency to think of persons as physical. But, as Jesus said: "God is spirit and those worshipping (Him) must worship (Him) as spirit and truth." (John 4:24.) Clearly, since YAHWEH is in no way physical, to impart sexual connotations to the pronoun as applied to Him is idolatrous and blasphemous. It belongs to an age of religious ideas long past, an age when humans knew no better.

As to the argument by feminists that YAHWEH must be considered feminine because spirit (Hebrew ruhca) in the Old Testament is feminine gender: this is so only because abstracts like love (ahabh) and the Hebrew word yirah (too often translated "fear") are feminine. Spirit is certainly an abstract concept. (Note also, in the New Testament, the dialogue in Matthew 16:18 where Jesus uses the masculine "rock" petros as the name for Peter and the same word in feminine gender petra in reference to Peter's confession.)

To resort to she in the cases where he has become common usage, is not very productive of accurate thought. It would be displacing a neutral word (sexually) with one that is definitely sexual. She needs no context for identification. He must always be modified by the context to get at its true meaning. I find it very difficult to think of YAHWEH in the neuter form of "it" as a pronoun. He is not a thing! He created all things. He is a person. Things designated by "it" are not persons. YAHWEH is a person, and we are made in His image whether male or female.

# Chapter 5

# YAHWEH
# The Sacred Name

For many, this is a strange word. But this is the case only because the earlier translations of the Old Testament into English followed the irrational superstition of the Masoretes. These scribes began to put vowel marks to the Hebrew script of the Old Testament around 700 C.E. (A.D.) They effectively blocked pronunciation of YAHWEH by using the vowels of the word adhonai (lord). This made the sacred name unpronounceable. A reference was then made in the margin instructing the reader to say adhonai. The superstition held that the unclean lips of humankind would soil the Name and so one should substitute "the Lord". The KJV and RSV translators indicated where this was done by capitalizing the entire word LORD.

It is unfortunate that this practice of substituting lord for YAHWEH was followed by the English translators. It led to much confusion in the New Testament and the Greek translation of the Old Testament. There only the Greek word kurios (lord) was available. Since only the Septuagint is quoted in the New Testament, there is no distinction between the use of YAHWEH and adhonai. And since the word lord is applied to Jesus as well as to YAHWEH, the two are often confused. New Testament quotations of Psalms and the prophets especially are made to refer to Jesus because YAHWEH is not distinguished in the Greek. Their roles are naively intermingled. This gives false support to the dogma introduced at Nicaea by the pagan emperor Constantine that Yahweh and Jesus are the same (homoousia), not just like (homoiousia) as scholars had established from the Bible.

The sacred name should not be strange to all those who frequently sing or say "Halleluia!" in their worship services. This is just the Hebrew word that means "Praise you YAHWEH!" (hallel=praise; u=you; ya=an abbreviated form of YAHWEH.)

Psalms 104 and 106 end with this Hebrew word. 106 and 111-113 begin with it. 117 begins and ends with halleluia although it does not have the abbreviated form at the beginning.

We have been done a disservice by the translators who followed the superstition of the Masoretes in substituting LORD for YAHWEH. In fact, it is a direct violation of the command issued in Exodus 3:14f.: "The Mighty One (eloheem) also was saying to Moses, 'I am being who I am being' Then He was saying, 'Thus you are saying to the sons of Israel:' "I Am Being has sent me to you." Then the Mighty One added, saying to Moses, 'Thus you are saying to the sons of Israel, "YAHWEH the Mighty One of your Fathers, the Strength of Abraham, the Power of Isaac and the Might of Jacob has sent me to you. This is my name forever and this is my remembrance for every generation."'"

The "Priestly Benediction" (Numbers 6:24-27) adds to this: "YAHWEH bless you and protect you. YAHWEH cause His face to shine upon you and favor you. YAHWEH lift up His face upon you and establish peace for you. 'So they have put my name upon the sons of Israel and I am blessing them.'"

The meaning of the name YAHWEH is found in Exodus 3:14. The verb forms in "I am being who I am being" (ehyeh asher ehyeh) are both Qal Imperfect, first person, singular. The sacred Name abbreviates and combines them into one word. To translate these verbs adequately into English would require many words—an attempt to describe the infinite which would be a contradiction in itself. How can one put a circle around (that is the meaning of "describe") the infinite?

The Imperfect verb form in Hebrew is unique in that it expresses a sort of flash picture of a subject moving along on a continuum. It is neither past, present nor future and yet may be any of these. Thus YAHWEH means "I am being what I am being" (He really is what He is revealing Himself to be.) "I will be what I was being" (He does not change.) "I will be being what I will be being" (He is all powerful, no one can inhibit or prevent the fulfillment of His will.) "I am being where I will be being" (His presence is as He chooses and, according to Jeremaih 23:23f., that means everywhere present.) See also the first two chapters of Jonah and Psalm 139:7-10.

One can go on making all the possible combinations. Each one says something about the Father-Creator. Each one verifies the nature of His infinite qualities. Thus we have a sacred representation of the only true infinite God YAHWEH. We humans who are like Him are nevertheless a little less as the creature is less than the Creator.

The clumsy attempt to translate or transliterate the impossible Hebrew combination of YAHWEH and the vowels of adhonai given in the KJV 6:3 of Exodus; Psalm 83:18 and Isaiah 12:2 and 26:4 is unjustified. Those who follow them are equally misguided. "Jehovah," is a reflection of the lack of understanding by those making this clumsy attempt to pronounce the unpronounceable.

YAHWEH is YAHWEH. This is how He is to be known by every generation.

# PART 2

## ABOUT THE CHURCH

# Chapter 6

# Creeds and Fragmentation of the Church and Synagogue

From a parochial view in defining a creed, the visible Christian Church usually thinks in terms of those such as the "Apostle's Creed" or Athanasian or Nicene creeds. It is this parochial view that has led to fragmentation of the Church. It was not long after Jesus was crucified that various creeds began to be used as a test of orthodoxy or heresy. In this sense, a creed is an accepted system of religious belief. When one is thereby required to recite and subscribe to such a creed as a test of acceptance or rejection by a religious group, freedom of thought and growth toward truth is hampered or even prohibited in that group.

By such means religious thought and growth are shut down. Among Jews, Moslems, Buddhists and Christians, the devastating, divisive effects of such creedalism is obvious. Not only are people who claim to be worshipping the same God driven apart, they even have done and are doing great physical violence to each other in the name of "defending the faith". Such atrocities always are rooted in an attempt to compel people to believe and think the way of the creed. All of this is an indication of spiritual dictatorship that leads to spiritual immaturity of both controllers and those controlled.

The writer of the epistle to the Hebrews gives a clear definition of religious maturity: "For everyone partaking of milk is inexperienced in the word of righteousness, for he is an infant. But solid food is for those who are mature (teleion, partitive genitive) through having had their faculties trained by practice to distinguish between good and evil." (Hebrews 5:13f.) The important words here are "experience" and "practice".

As Jesus practiced all that he preached and so validated his own teachings, so we grow up in love (ahabh and agape) only by sharing experiences of loving and by the obligations of love fulfilled. No one has the verbal genius to describe or to make another acquainted with this kind of love by words alone. But by experiencing and practicing, love is known and made known to others. If ever there was a basis for a useful creed, that would be it. And that would be the first step to knowing and becoming one with our Father-Creator.

However, since an honest creed can never be more than an individual's testimony of his own experience of God, it is not possible properly for any one person or group to produce a written or other formal statement that can fairly be required of others. Not even our Father-Creator will invade the spiritual freedom of His children in such an abominable fashion. As an illustration of His appraisal of creeds, Isaiah 29:13 reports YAHWEH as saying: "Because this people draw near with his (their) mouth and with his (their) lips honor me, yet his heart is far from me and their reverence of me is a commandment of men trained (as an ox to the yoke)." (Cf. Hosea 10:11 where the same word (melummadhah) is used.

In Exodus 3:15, we find Moses instructed: "Thus you are saying to the children of Israel: 'YAHWEH, the God of your fathers...has sent me to you. This is my name always and this is my memorial for every generation.'" The responsibility of the informed is to make the infinite YAHWEH known. But no one is compelled to accept or subscribe to this great truth. Even the first part of the creed of Judaism (Deuteronomy 6:4-9) is in no way given as a basis for heresy trials or for ostracism. Rather, it is a command to make known the way of atonement. Each one is left free to choose to accept or reject that love—to love or not to love.

The immature have only been taught. The mature have applied what they have been taught and can, therefore, testify to their experience of a loving, provident, Father-Creator. They can say: "YAHWEH is a mighty One, compassionate and gracious, patient and the very being of steadfast love and truth." (Exodus 34:6.) But how in His creation can one possibly presume to demand of any other human the same testimony if that person has not chosen to "taste and see that YAHWEH is good." (tobh, Psalm 34:8, verse 9 in Hebrew.) Those who have, will gladly and voluntarily proclaim His greatness and His goodness. Like Paul, they can proclaim "We know that to those loving God, He works together into good all things..." (Romans 8:28.)

Be assured, I am not referring (as I am certain Paul was not) to a sentimental but empty verbal assertion or commitment. Love of God and man, when practiced, produces a maturity that makes clear to the laborers in the Kingdom of God what is true and what is false.

Formal creeds imposed by powerful potentates like the pagan Constantine at Nicaea or by some parochial group such as the rabbis who gave us the Mishnah and Talmud, or the College of Cardinals, the Westminster Assembly or any other religious or secular assembly tend only to divide. Surely, they fail at atonement. History and the current fragmentation of Judaism, Christianity, and Buddhist and Muslim religions show this to be true.

A creed ought not to be some statement we demand of others or that all must participate in ritually. It should not be used in witch hunts or heresy trials. The true creed should be always and only one's own testimony of his personal experience of God. An example can be found in the fact that Jesus of Nazareth never set up a single creed such as subsequent men have established in their rituals and as tests of orthodoxy. He never demanded any proclamation from any one. He did, however, make some very bold statements that were expressive of his own experience of the Father. He said that God's love never ceases even from those who turn away from Him. He said that that love is the power of forgiveness for truly repentant souls (e.g., Luke 15.) He showed that the Father is a constant source of comfort and strength to those experiencing trials. To this end Jesus, on the cross, referred his followers to Psalms 22 and 31.

The reason for all this is that Jesus was far too busy listening to the Father for guidance, and then obeying instructions, to be involved in setting up creeds and dogmas that bind others to a religious community or exclude them from it. He had no need for formal statements to be recited in public. His method was always to invite others to come and join him in a life of loving the lovable Father and all His children (some not so lovable.)

Note also that when Jesus acknowledges the Two Great Commandments as pre-eminent and as the means of atonement or the heavenly life (Luke 10:25-28), he never even hinted that the words spoken by the scribe were to be recited or made a creed of any sort. Ho only said: "This do and you shall live." (Luke 10:28.)

Jesus' creeds (if they can be called that) were the standards by which he lived. They were those things that expressed his inner being—those things that worked out in his daily life. I.e., he lived them and proclaimed them with his life. This is precisely where creeds belong: a creed should be what we proclaim by the way we live. It should not be what we proclaim with our lips and demand of others as a condition of fellowship. A creed should be what we demand of ourselves, although we may speak it in explanation of why we live as we do.

# Chapter 7

# Ritual to Rote to Paganism-- Habit in Human Nature

One of the basic differences between humans and animals (or beasts) is that animals are governed by instinct while humans are governed by habit. I suppose the reason for this difference is mainly that man has a more highly developed intellect so that he manages to overrule his instincts by reason and subsequently establishes habits. The Old Testament Prophet Jeremiah reports the words of YAHWEH: "Can the Cushite alter his skin or the leopard (tiger) his stripes? So also you are able to be good who are accustomed to being evil." (Jeremiah 13:23.) This would make habit an irrevocable state, hopeless and helpless of correction or change.

But, like much of prophecy, Jeremiah is resorting to hyperbole for the sake of effect. He is trying to impress the people with the depth to which all have fallen in corruption—kings, priests, prophets and people. The day of YAHWEH has arrived. He is fed up with their stubborn insensitivity to His will which is solely for their welfare. It is clear that the only way He can get their attention is to change their status sufficiently to cleanse them of their accumulated bad habits.

Jesus looks at habits somewhat differently. Luke records the parable of a man from whom an unclean spirit has been purged. (Luke 11:24-26.) The implication is that habits cannot just be eliminated. They must be replaced by better ones or worse habits flow into the vacuum.

## About The Church

It appears that we have to be governed by habit to a large degree. Without habit, we shall be overwhelmed by the need to make again and again so many little choices in our daily life that there is no time left for those things truly important. Suppose each morning we had to decide which side of the bed to get out of, which foot or hand to put forth for each stage of getting dressed. whether to start at the bottom or the top to button a garment, (fortunately sometimes zippers eliminate that one) whether to start at the top or the bottom with our bath or shower, on and on all day long.

Even weightier matters can trip us up if we have no principles, which are a habitual way of thinking. Should I try to return a valuable lost item I have found or keep it? Should I respond in kind to others who irritate me or be a better example? If we have not replaced the "unclean spirit" in this regard by one under the principle of love, we shall be known as one of poor character. It is the quality of the habit that determines which way we shall behave. If the "house" is vacant, we may agonize over such decisions and others much more important.

In regard to religious behavior, a habit becomes ritual. When ritual in worship becomes rote, worship can well be pagan. Too often people in a church or synagogue, or other place of worship, are slavishly following habit instilled in childhood. It may be a routine picked up in fellowship with others. In any case, if each habit has not been carefully evaluated from time to time, it can well be an "unclean spirit"—a thoughtless practice that may be even pagan idolatry. We need not be hopelessly overwhelmed by constant self-evaluation, but it pays to take time occasionally to examine why we do what we do in relationship with others and especially with our Father-Creator. How else shall we hear what He is trying to say to us so as to improve our lives and our loves.?

Some marvelous effects upon history have been made by habitual behavior of persons. The Maccabees laid their lives on the line because of their habit of devotion to faithfulness to the will of YAHWEH as they knew it. It was the same devotion that preserved the Jewish religion down through the ages when so many great powers labored to stamp it out. The habit of loyalty to their concept of YAHWEH worship at Masada led to a climactic witness seldom seen in religious loyalty. Heroes are generally not given time for meditation before committing an heroic act. It is their

*Ritual to Rote to Paganism--Habit in Human Nature*

habitual responses that control in a crisis. In such cases, taking time to evaluate a situation would mean the passing of an opportunity for heroics. So it is that those entrusted with piloting passenger planes or with fire or police protection daily perform heroic acts. They are intensively trained to make their responses habitual. Their attitude must originally be altruistic. The best of them are idealistic persons. These are qualities of character that must become habitual or they will not work in a crisis since instincts will force the person to seek self-preservation.

When it comes to worship, however, when habitual ritual becomes rote, the mind is similarly put in neutral. True worship must be conscious and deliberate. The first principle of all Judaeo-Christians is "YAHWEH is our Strength. YAHWEH is one. So you shall love YAHWEH your God with all your mind, with all your soul and with all your being." It is not possible to love without purposeful, vivid, total devotion of consciousness. There is no place for either habit or instinct here. No doubt this is why we do not think of animals at worship. These are qualities, a gift of God for our convenience. But the image of God in humans, makes it possible to transcend the beast in us, is given to overcome control by habit or instinct.

Much of our life is controlled by habit. Habits established from proper ideals can contribute to efficient and good social behavior and so are vitally important. But worship is a unique category of living. It is there that ideals are developed and our habits reviewed and judged. Our religion is the means by which we form and improve our habits that make living what it ought to be. Much of our life is lived by habit. But ultimately we choose what those habits shall be. It is very important that we have the true standard for exercising that right of choice. YAHWEH is His Name. If, like Jesus, the son of the carpenter of Nazareth, we carefully and constantly seek to conform to that standard, we too shall leave the world a better place because we have been here. Our habits will be good and getting better.

# Chapter 8

# Of Priests and Clergy

Ivory tower religious philosophy (mental gymnastics, sometimes called "theology") is simply a means of perpetuating the arrogance of the definition of priests and clergy as "stewards of the mysteries of God." It is the same method used by witch doctors, kahunas and voodoo priests to keep their privileged role in a society.

In the Bible, the only persons who were not forced to sell themselves to Pharaoh under Joseph's administration in the seven years of drought and famine were the priests. Upon the return of the tribe of Jacob to the Holy Land, the books of Exodus and Numbers assured the families of Aaron and Levi a secure economic status by means of goodly portions of obligatory offerings and town and land plots assigned to them in perpetuity.

Once more, the priests guaranteed their privileges under a favorable King Josiah after a period of long neglect. The book of Deuteronomy re-established those privileges and ordered horrible curses on the nation if there was a failure to comply with the full ritual religion upon which the priests depended for their livelihood.

Then again, upon return of the captives from Babylon, the priests laid down a new constitution in the book of Leviticus. No longer were they dependent upon a favorable monarchy. In a way, this was a return

## About The Church

to the religio-political control similar to the time of their flight from Egypt seven or eight hundred years earlier. It was a new dispensation as noted by the prophet Jeremiah: "Therefore, behold, the days are coming, says YAHWEH, when it shall no longer be said, 'As YAHWEH lives who brought up the people of Israel out of the land of Egypt,' but 'As YAHWEH lives who brought up the people of Israel out of the north country and out of all of the countries where He had driven them...'" (Jeremiah 23:7f.) The priestly families would then be in control of all facets of life in the temple colony. It was a new law, similar in many ways to that of Exodus and Numbers, but unique in that there was no Moses or Joshua and no king. Having both economic and political control of the colony, priests and Levites were then guaranteed economic security.

If you bring this down to the Christian era, from Constantine onward, we see very similar goings on in the "Church". Inventing a mystery only comprehensible or explainable by "theologians," guarantees their ceonomic security. Of course, they make innumerable futile attempts to make sense of the nonsense of the "trinity."

The homely explanations, that always fail to satisfy the laity for long, indicate how highly they perceive of their insights and how lowly they perceive of the capacity of the laity. If one says one and three are distinct and yet (in regards to the trinity) they are the same, the theologians are not really being profound or producing a paradox or a mystery, as they sometimes say, but, in a very real sense, they are destroying language. When words just mean the same thing—they really mean nothing.

When the still pagan Constantine took over the Church at the Council of Nicaea and demanded the use of the word homoousia rather than homoiousia (as had been agreed upon by Bible scholars), he laid the foundation for all the subsequent controversy and confusion that has prevailed to this day among Christians. If Jesus is the "same as" God, how is it God raised him from the dead? How is it that Jesus sits at the right hand of God? How can the father also be the son and the son the father? The so-called stewards of the mysteries of God administer the answers and so guard their sanctified role in human society—but only so long as people are not allowed to resort to good common sense (true inspiration). That is to say, as long as their right to think is fenced in by creeds and

*Of Priests and Clergy*

dogmas created by parochial assemblies of theologians.

There is a very vital role for Christian clergy. That is the role of teacher and leader in Bible study. Naturally, no craftsman would think of going to work without the tools of his trade. Anyone who would be a carpenter certainly must be willing to learn effective use of saw, plane, hammer and compass. Other craftsmen must likewise learn each the tools of his trade.

So a teacher and leader of Bible study must learn the original languages of Hebrew, Aramaic and Greek in which the Bible was written. He or she must also be willing to come to know well the history of the origin of the Bible and how it came to its present form. Anyone who does less should not be allowed the privileges of this service. As the writer of the epistle of James put it: "Let not many of you seek to become teachers:...for you know that we who teach shall be judged with greater strictness." (James 3:1.)

Since all that is necessary for a wholesome society and a full and good individual life is to be found in the Bible—it is hardly necessary that clergy be specialists (or craftsmen) in any other subject to qualify for their proper privileges.

If such specialists stimulate us to think and to evaluate our lives so that we grow spiritually, they have justified their vocation. But, in no way dare we permit them to substitute their thinking for our own or to substitute their communication with the Father-Creator for our own. Theirs is the task of learning and teaching as accurately as possible what the Bible says in the original languages. It is to help us to evaluate the differences in the many translations put upon us. But it is you and I who must find the Word of God in it in our own understanding as we seek with all our minds to know the only true God. No one can do that for us.

# PART 3

# ON RELIGIOUS COMMUNICATION

# Chapter 9

# On Prophecy and the "Word"

In a review of the entire Bible, one will find that what is meant by the "word" of YAHWEH mainly applies to an expression of His will. The "Thus says YAHWEH..." does not always come out right, for the prophet and his hearers are always fallible humans. So the message may well be only an expression of the will of the person speaking or of the society. One, at this point, might throw up his hands in frustration. It would seem that the "word" is beyond reach. But, since cause and effect is part of revelation, prejudice can be filtered out effectively.

A good example of this is to be found in the choice by the people Israel of a king. "And YAHWEH said to Samuel, 'Listen to the voice of the people in all that they say to you; for they have not rejected you, but they have rejected me from being king over them.'" (I Samuel 8:7.) Even the great ethical prophets (Isaiah, Amos, Hosea and Micah) appear to accept a king as appropriate. In their historical position it was not yet clear that, beginning with Saul the first Messiah and on throughout the history of the monarchy, this interposition of any man between them and YAHWEH led to devastating consequences. (This applies to the use of intercessory priests as well. Compare chapter 8 - Of Priests and Clergy.)

The opening of the mind of an individual to YAHWEH personally and directly makes the coming of inspiration possible. By this means alone does the Spirit of YAHWEH in-dwell an individual. As it is written in Deuteronomy 4:29, speaking of YAHWEH: "...you have found Him for you are searching after Him with all your mind and with all your soul." (See also Jeremiah 29:13.) One must be honest, observant, sincere and devoting the ultimate of one's mental faculties to hear the "word". If we desire to know the word of YAHWEH, it is quite clear that we shall have to give our best times to listening. These times may be such as the peak of our bio-rythmic cycles. And yet, we know how crises often stir us to acute mental perceptibility.

We also learn from experience that, in the dead of night, solutions to frustrating or perplexing problems often come. As the psalmist said it: "Be still and know that I am God..." (Psalm 46:10.) There is some truth in the saying that YAHWEH is present everywhere except in the unreceptive soul. He will not infringe upon the right He has given to us, each one, to exclude Him. But neither will He fail to respond to those who sincerely seek Him as He is. As Jesus said: "God is spirit, and those worshipping Him must worship Him as spirit and truth." (John 4:24.)

The word of YAHWEH comes to humans in many ways. It is not as an animist who stubs his toe on a stone and feels that the spirit in it is crying to be carried some distance to a new place. But one may be incited to remove the stone to make the path smooth for others who follow. It may come in any experience. It may be like the two baskets of figs before the prophet Jeremiah (24:1ff.) He sees the good and bad figs as representing separation of the obedient and disobedient in the consequences meted out in the Babylonian conquest and captivity of Israel.

Ezekiel (1:1ff.) and Isaiah (6:1ff.) in the time of depression under events overwhelming to each of them; each one has a breath-taking visionary experience of the transcendent magnificence of the Creator. This is not unlike the poet who gave us the book of Job. His careful observation of the world around him as well as of the works of mankind, filled him with awe for YAHWEH and His concern for justice toward all humans. All these have heard the word.

Psalm 8 speaks of the glory and majesty of YAHWEH revealed in His creation. Psalm 19 speaks of YAHWEH telling of His glory and His creative acts by means of the magnificent universe. Order in His creation is a constant revelation of Himself. Psalm 29:3-9 says YAHWEH'S voice is heard in thunder and the storms that tear at the sea and forests. It is like this that any thoughtful person hears the Father say in a lovely flower, sunrise or sunset: "I love you." Love elicited from us at the sight of any infant creature is another way that He speaks of His love. In the effects of our thoughts and actions upon ourselves and others, He tells us what is right and what is wrong. If one will but learn to listen, while being conscious of our Father-Creator's constant attention, he finds that YAHWEH is speaking to us everywhere and at all times. As the poet says in the hymn "This is My Father's World": "In the rustling grass I hear Him pass, He speaks to me everywhere." (Rev. Maltbie D. Babcock, 1901.) We too can be prophets if only we listen for His word.

The Hebrew word translated "prophet" means exactly the same as the English word: to speak forth. In the noun form it means spokesman. A prophet of YAHWEH is one who serves as a mouth for YAHWEH who is spirit and therefore must communicate with the unlearned on earth through His creatures and His creation. All truth is YAHWEH'S truth. Therefore all spoken truth is prophecy. It is not limited to forecasting as some usages of the word indicate. Prophecy can be evaluation or judgment in the past, present, or the future. This would make true science, as well as religion, prophecy. Science speaks of "HOW" religion speaks of "WHO" and "WHY". When true, both are equally the word—prophecy. At this point, there would be no distinction between secular and sacred. The true word is always sacred—that is, prophecy. All those who speak it are prophets.

So we are able to know what in the Bible is truly the word—truly prophecy. The whole history of humanity has borne testimony to the validity of the second of the Two Great Commandments. "When a stranger dwells with you in the land, you shall not do him wrong. The stranger who dwells with you shall be to you as a native among you, and you shall love him as yourself..." (Leviticus 19:33f.) Failure to do so has brought calamity to many individuals and so to society itself.

Another example, look to the description of the character of YAHWEH as stated in Exodus 34:6: YAHWEH is YAHWEH, a mighty one compassionate and gracious, patient and the very substance of steadfast love and truth." All those who carefully look and listen know this to be true. It cannot be known just from the words of another. One has to hear their senses speak. (Note chapter 35 - I Believe Because.) Love, however, is experienced first from parents and siblings. If it is not learned there, one may find great difficulty in ever coming to know the meaning of this word.

Those who are violent and antisocial in any society testify to this. Those dealing with their rehabilitation especially know it.

As with religion, so with science: if it works, it is true, at least in that set of circumstances. One knows love by loving and being loved. Experience teaches the virtue of patience. One gets to understand others by experiencing compassion. When one knows these things, he can understand why the Creator is like that and why He has made us like Himself. When we put such knowledge into words, we prophesy.

# Chapter 10

# Ways YAHWEH Speaks

"The sacred writings...are able to instruct you into salvation..." (II Timothy 3:15.) Of course, the Bible like any other book does not really speak. But it is through books that authors speak to people of this world. When anyone speaks the truth, he is a prophet—a speaker or voice for YAHWEH. The writer of the epistle to Timothy (in the context of the words quoted above) says that it is "through faith in Christ Jesus all scripture is God inspired..." (verses 15f.) So some touchstones must be applied or the message from the Bible becomes distorted and misleading. Thus cautions the writer of the First Epistle of John: "Beloved, do not believe every spirit (inspiration), but examine the spirits (inspirations) [to know] if they are from God..." (I John 4:1.)

The Bible is the means by which YAHWEH speaks to all mankind through the servants He used to preserve discovered truths there written. The weakness of this kind of communication is in the fact that people have to choose to come to the Bible. It is my experience that few will give the time necessary really to get to know it. Knowing the whole Bible is the work of a lifetime. As I noted in chapter 1 - On Scripture in General, all that mankind has ever thought about the nature of God, man, creation and our relationship to each other is included in the Bible. That means that all the true things as well as all the false things humans have ever thought regarding religion are there.

Jesus of Nazareth gave a clear presentation by which anyone is able to sort out what is true and what is false among these ideas. One must be sensitive to what goes on around him and to what has been revealed in the cause-effect results of history. These also are ways by which the Father-Creator speaks to us. In our day of radio and T.V., our ears are constantly pounded by words, words and more words. Many of these are meant to worm their way into our subconscious so that our decisions are controlled by them. If we are not alert, we may well be led in directions we do not wish to go. Still, we do have full freedom to acquiesce to such pressure or to examine and filter all such influences so breathed into our subconsciousness. This is not easy, but the Father is there too, knocking, and we need to be vigilant so as to hear Him. True religion has no place for lazy minds.

There is one way to check on what has infiltrated our minds so subtly. It hangs mainly on examining our habits. Why do we do what we do and why that way? Habits are necessary. But they can be either good or bad. If we had to evaluate every routine act every time, we would have little left to give to those things that require our full attention. (See chapter 7 - Ritual to Rote to Paganism...) We need some quiet times to undertake such examinations—regularly. It is surprising how many different relevant subjects pop into our minds while reading or sharing the Bible. Look into the Mishnah and Talmud and see the myriad thoughts that spring off single words of Scripture as the rabbis share in its study. It can happen to you and to me also. We must be careful not to read into the Bible things that are not there. But it is inevitable that, whatever we are reading there, might turn up thoughts of some practical or moral matter before us. That is the way Bible study and sharing works. The Father speaks in His written word.

Elihu, the true hero of the book of Job, having patiently respected the age of Job and his three friends, has listened for some proper answers for Job's difficulties. Since none are forthcoming, he proclaims that the wisdom of age is not productive in this case. He says: "But in fact it is spirit (ruhca) in mankind (enosh), the breath (neshamah) of the Almighty [that] is causing them to understand." (Job 32:8.)

Useful understanding of a truth is God's Mind expressing itself in our minds. Those used to close personal association with the Father know this as the most real and vivid experience of communication with Him. For those not having had this experience because they have been unfamiliar with or insensitive to the word, this is the most mysterious and difficult to accept. It is nearly impossible to discuss this form of communication with those who have never listened to the prompting of the Spirit-God who is always there. Still, all have known a certain amount of what is called ESP with close family members or associates. Everyone very close to another person frequently knows the thoughts of the other before they have been spoken. So it is with us when we remain close to the Father.

Questions arrive in our minds that have no background of experience that can explain them. It is simply the way the Father calls our attention to a blank spot in our knowledge that needs filling. That is the way it is it is with doubts. As there is no such thing as a bad or foolish sincere question, so there is no bad doubt. Both are opportunities for edification. Doubts are calls from the Spirit-God Mind to mind, to turn our attention to a weakness in our faith. Among the collected sayings of Jesus recorded in Matthew, Jesus says, "Blessed are those hungering and thirsting for righteousness. They shall be completely filled." (Matthew 5:6.) As it is written in Deuteronomy—speaking of the disobedient people exiled for their waywardness—when they have had enough and they turn back to YAHWEH: "From there, having sought YAHWEH your God, you will have found Him because you were seeking Him with all your mind and with all your soul." (4:29.) Nothing less brings true revelation to fruit in us.

As our Father-Creator speaks in Scripture and in questions and doubts, so also He is and has been speaking in diversions or crises that we experience. Take for example what we experience in bereavement. So frequently we begin to regret having failed to express love more often toward the deceased loved one. One, listening for our Father's wisdom, will discover a call to show that love to those still with us. It may also reveal to us the need to treat each moment as though it might be the last so as not to put off being and doing what we know to be right. Then we shall be freed of all concern for the future. This is part of the means of attaining the peace that surpasses all understanding.

The near tragedy of the "Prodigal Son" (Luke 15) is a classic presentation of the experience of many parents. How strongly is taught the value and purpose of forgiveness. How richly love flows when a parent with an aching heart sees seeds sown in childhood bring a grown child back from the brink of a wrecked life. In this parable, we also learn why the Father forgives. The lovely experience that comes to us in the act of forgiveness makes us know. He is speaking quite clearly to us in such times in our lives on earth.

How vividly do we hear Him speak in consequences of our own behavior! We see the multitude of ailments that are produced by such things as gluttony, sexual promiscuity, improper use of drugs (including alcohol and tobacco), covetousness and jealousy. Our bodies are a stewardship for which we must always give an accounting eventually. But what happens to us in such abuses are merely warnings, i.e., disciplinary rather than punitive (depending upon how we take it.) In His love, the Father cannot take away our freedom of choice or there could be no love in us. So He is constantly providing us opportunities to hear what He is saying . And so we are taught in love.

In regard to war, the writer of the epistle of James says: "From where comes wars and from where are fightings among you? Are they not out of your lusts that there are battles among your members? You covet and do not have. You murder and wage war..." (James 4:1f.) Much is said here that is plain condemnation of covetousness that is the cause of wars between both individuals and societies. We have many years of plain speaking about the evils of war. We know all the harmful effects of war. We see moral degradation, waste, hunger, disease and many other ills that always accompany or follow. It is odd that, with all the means that humans have of preserving and presenting history, that mankind has not yet learned from what the Father-Creator is saying in and about it.

This also may be why the futility of plenty, as a main goal or final achievement, is not clearly perceived. So many people in need seem to feel that the answer to all their desires is to be rich in material things. If humans could only be satisfied with enough, (what makes one most efficient in achieving good health and mental equilibrium) covetousness would not so dominate them. We see that very few people who attain great wealth are truly blessed. There is prophecy in the words of Proverbs 30:8f.: "...neither poverty nor riches give to me; cause me to eat bread decreed for me (my share) lest I have abundance and deny thee...or lest

I be poor and steal and do violence to the name of my God." As Jesus said, it is not easy for one to have great wealth and still be loyal to the Father-Creator. (Mark 10:23.) He did not say that it is impossible. But as with teaching—it takes special persons to be able constructively to accept so great a responsibility.

Nero, Napoleon, Hitler, Stalin all help us to hear what the Father is saying about humans who usurp His role of dominance over mankind. We have all known "little Hitlers" and heard the message loud and clear. Great hurts come when people do not listen. Elihu says it beautifully in that ballad poem, Job 33:12-30. It is well worth reading here.

# Chapter 11

## Communication--Prayer--Incantations--"Tongues"

"Solomon stood to the front of the altar of YAHWEH in the sight of all the assembly of Israel and he spread out his hands the heavens and prayed..." (I Kings 8:22f.) At other places in the Old Testament we find petitioners just prostrating themselves. Other places we find that the attitude is not mentioned as though posture was not important. Similarly in the New Testament, as Jesus prays in Gethsemane, Mark 14:35 says Jesus fell on the ground and prayed. Luke says he knelt down (Luke 22:41.) Matthew says he fell on his face (Matthew 26:39.) In the long prayer of Jesus recorded in John 17:1ff., the writer says he lifted up his eyes to heaven (verse 1.) In Jesus' instructions regarding manners in prayer, he cautions his disciples against ostentation in worship. He says: "But when you pray, go into your chamber (closet) and shut the door and pray..." (Matthew 6:6.)

Generally speaking, the Bible does not emphasize any particular attitude of body in prayer. After all, when Paul says that we should pray constantly (I Thessalonians 5:17), it is hardly possible that he visualized his followers going about on their knees with hands clasped and their eyes directed heavenward all the time. This would, at the very least, make it a world hard to get around in! Safely!

## On Religious Communication

Since the Father-Creator is Spirit and is everywhere present (except in unreceptive souls), the writer of the 139th Psalm proclaims that YAHWEH knows completely what we are thinking even before we are clear on it ourselves. Under these circumstances, it is hardly likely that we will surprise Him with any new insights. Since He is all knowing, there is no possibility that we shall be able to show Him ways of improving His creation or of making our individual lot better than it is. As Jesus said: "Do not seek what you are to eat and what you are to drink and do not be anxious minded (meteoridzo)...your Father knows that you need them." (Luke 12:29f.) Obviously our Father knows not only what we need, but what we want also.

It seems at this point that any attempt to inform the Creator of anything is redundant. Any clamor for gifts from Him, Luke 18:1-7 notwithstanding, is useless. Surely, He knows much better than we do what we need to be the kind of person each of us ought to be and what kinds of experiences are needed for us to achieve that end. The parable of the judge who yields to demands of a widow only because she threatens to wear him out with her persistence is hardly a comforting picture of YAHWEH! It is the picture of a beleaguered parent who spoils a child by giving in to whining and tugging on her apron strings or his coat tails. The motive is not justice. It is self-protection or relief that would be akin to adults accepting bribes and other forms of questionable persuasion that influence only weak persons. It hardly qualifies as a spiritual approach to an infinite, all-wise God.

If it is redundant to ask the Father for things, and if there is no way to tell Him what He does not already know, that pretty well excludes most of what we are encouraged to do in prayer both in the church doctrines and in the New Testament itself. What is left? Note the inconsistencies of the gospels regarding the reports of what Jesus said about praying. It is my conviction that a man who had such a great and lasting influence on all the religions of the world could not have been inconsistent. The contradictory reports on what he said therefore, must be attributed to incorrect reporting by those who wrote about him. After all it was more than 30 years after his death when the first gospel was written as we have it. Reports passed by word of mouth change considerably in a short time.

In any contradiction, one or both sides have to be wrong. It is clear,

## Communication--Prayer--Incantations--"Tongues"

then, that we shall have to struggle with the gospels to try to find what Jesus really did say about prayer, as well as about anything else. Perhaps some sense of direction can be found in knowing that Jesus uses the Two Great Commandments as the center of all religious behavior and of truth about God, man, and the relationship between them. We need also to be reminded of his dependence upon the Old Testament and his saying that our Father knows what we need before we can ask Him.

It is proper therefore to test every rendering of his sayings by the two questions: (1) Does it manifest love of God and love of His creatures and His creation? (2) Does it square with the maturer Old Testament understanding of the completeness of YAHWEH'S knowledge of what goes on in the minds of His children? (Consider particularly Psalm 139 and Jeremiah 23:23f.)

To communicate with the Father is (1) being gratefully and happily conscious of the nature of His presence and (2) lovingly listening to what He is saying. That is nearly the sum total of prayer. A true Jew or Christian will know from the Bible (the word of YAHWEH) and, from all of creation as it impinges upon our consciousness, not only the magnificence of YAHWEH, but even more so His infinite love. This will mean that the true believer will rejoice in the knowledge of the constant presence and attention of God. We shall not be fearful that the Father-Creator is constantly watching over our shoulder. We shall know that He knows our every thought and deed and be glad of it.

This points up the most important part of prayer—gratitude. Praying constantly, then, means above all constantly giving thanks—at least being thankful. We have all heard of the two perspectives of a glass one-half filled: (l) It is one-half full. (2) It is one-half empty. This illustrates the two choices before every human. We can always look to the positive side of each circumstance or event in our lives; we can always look at the down side. Perhaps no historical character, other than Jesus himself, suffered more for his discipleship than Paul. (Note II Corinthians 11:23-29.) Still he could say with fervor, "for those loving God, He works all things into good..." (Romans 8:28.)

When the bereaved lament, thinking, "Why did God allow this to happen to me?" or when one says of illness or misfortune, "I must have done something terrible for God to do this to me." that person is not thinking of the true nature of our Father-Creator. Such a one needs to review the content of Psalm 22 to which Jesus referred those lamenting his crucifixion. For this psalm picks up a person who has temporarily blotted out of his mind the consistent providential care and concern of the Father. It carries him back to remembrance of YAHWEH'S past loving providence. It opens his eyes to current blessings overshadowed by the current crisis. It restores to the mind once more, assurance that the Father still cares and is still in charge of our true welfare.

The relevant question in any crisis for a true Judaeo-Christian person will always be, "Father, what good are you preparing me for in this experience?" God always sends good answers to this attitude of gratitude and confidence. Some answers will be: how one may be better equipped to help others, what are the proper priorities or values for a truly happy life in this world and how one may stand more effectively against evil. Morbid mourning, on the other hand, feeds on itself. It is paralyzing and destructive.

A good form of mourning leads one to positive actions that makes him a more loving person and more helpful to others in need. As Paul so well said it, "Blessed be the God...of all consolation (paraklaseos) who consoles us in all our afflictions so that we might be able to console those in any affliction with the consolation with which God has consoled us." (II Corinthians 1:3f.) Love begets good actions, not paralysis or debilitating depression. Prayer in such a case is listening because one feels gratitude and knows the Father will speak in or through the event as He does in all our experiences.

So we have come to the other side of communication: our thoughts directed to God. This should be the means of moving us to our own Gethsemane: "Father, not my will but thine be done." So we are properly responding as expected in the first of the Two Great Commandments. (Deuteronomy 6:4-9.) On account of gratitude, we shall respond in total love and obedience as an individual and as part of our family and community.

If we love our neighbors as ourselves, then we shall be grateful and rejoice for their blessings as much as for our own. One can never covet or feel jealousy with such love. If our neighbor suffers loss or pain or is threatened with danger, our love going out to him will strengthen him.

## Communication--Prayer--Incantations--"Tongues"

This is not a prayer of intercession, (in the churchly sense) for who needs an intercessor with a loving God who is constantly in attendance upon each one of us? But we can be used by the Father when we let His infinite love flow through us to another. He has granted us this service to one another in His command to love our neighbor. Such love may take the form of practical actions on our part or it may be only a spiritual boost for the other who is the object of our concern when circumstances make actions impossible. Love is a powerful force for healing mind and body, both ours and others'. The supply is infinite "...for God is Love." (I John 4:8.)

As the writer of Psalm 50 observes, sacrifice, incantations, confessions and such are most certainly not appropriate forms of worship of YAHWEH. This is especially true of hypocritical confessions of YAHWEH'S statutes or His covenant. The psalmist concludes for the Mighty One, YAHWEH: "To the one having offered thanksgiving and who set his way [right], I am showing salvation with Power (eloheem.)" (Psalm 50:16 and 23.) Jesus said, "In praying, you should not repeat words as the unbelievers do, for they think that by their many words they will be heard." (Matthew 6:7.)

Incantations, like mystery rituals, are serviceable for witch doctors, and holy magicians for impressing humans. It is inconceivable that any human creature could compel or even impel the Creator by any such action or word formula of any kind. These are much the same as church rituals such as the various forms of baptism, communion, bowing, standing, sitting, creedal statements, or music responses that some people feel are necessary for worship. They may help one who believes in them to get into a particular mood. They are not likely to have much effect upon the Creator. As YAHWEH Himself says to Samuel: "...YAHWEH sees not as man sees, for man (adam) looks to the eyes (appearance?) but YAHWEH looks to the mind. (labhabh.) (I Samuel 16:7.)

Speaking in "tongues" as it appeared in the Church, at least from Paul's time, is likely a state of auto-hypnosis. But I have known people who could turn it on and off like water from a faucet. When the ability to speak in "tongues" in this sense leads the person to a much more loving life, no fault can be found with it. Perhaps this is why Paul gives limited approval to it. But as a means of communicating with man or God, it is of no value. As Paul says, "...in church I would prefer to speak five words with my mind, in order to get through to others, than a myriad of words in a tongue." (I Corinthians 14:18.) In this context, he recognizes that speaking in tongues only serves the individual and any other human who may be moved by it. It has nothing at all to do with communicating with YAHWEH, for that requires clear, specific and sincere expressions of gratitude, love and obedience or submission.

All this being so: what is to be said about the so-called "Lord's Prayer" as it is frequently used? First of all, the title cannot fit because of the radical difference between what Jesus is reported to have said in Luke 11:2-4 and the accumulated additions ten years or so later in Matthew 6:9-13. No one can know from these passages what Jesus actually did say in answer to the request, "Teach us to pray." On the basis of all the reports we have of what Jesus said and demonstrated by example, one would have to change the ritual prayer as used in the Church to read as follows:

>Our Father who art in heaven,
>Holy is thy name (person).
>Thy Kingdom comes by thy will being done
>On earth as it is in heaven.
>You give us each day bread for the day.
>You forgive us our debts
>As we forgive those offending us.
>You do not lead us into temptation
>But you deliver us from evil. (Psalm 143:2.)
>So, thine is the Kingdom and the power
>And the glory for ever. Amen.

Having thought about these words and reviewing the full meaning of them, we might then feel we have worshipped through:

(1) Recognition of YAHWEH'S infinite nature.

(2) Having acknowledged His constant providence and loving care.

(3) Submitting ourselves to His will in love as a response to His

## *Communication--Prayer--Incantations--"Tongues"*

love.

(4) We make Him King by choosing to be His subjects.

But to memorize any prayer so that we can recite it without attending intensively and specifically to the meaning of each word is hardly worship. It may well even be pagan. It is no better than placing a written prayer in a prayer wheel and expecting it to be fired off to God with each turn of the wheel.

# Chapter 12

## Passing on the True Religion

It has been said that Christianity is always within one generation of extinction. This can be said just as well of any other religion. Aside from the possibility that some copies of the Bible would survive, the statement is correct. Humans are the only creatures that have the privilege of so long a period in which children are dependent.

We know, due to long stretches of sacrificial study of elephants and primates by certain dedicated individuals, that these creatures have sometimes almost as long periods in which their young are dependent upon adults as humans. However, no one has yet discovered elephants or primates developing intricate cultural, historical or religious traditions. None have been discovered writing books and keeping libraries so that knowledge from past generations could be made available to subsequent generations.

It is a human privilege to be able to assimilate all the wisdom of ages past early enough in the life of the individual to be able to add to what has accumulated already. Religious stewardship requires that we not spend all of our time in the past. As the writer of the epistle of Hebrews said: "Therefore, let us leave the teachings of the origin of the Christ that we may achieve maturity, not laying again a foundation from dead works and of faith toward God, instructions about baptisms, the laying on of hands, the resurrection of the dead, and eternal judgment." (Hebrews 6:1f.)

Had mankind devoted itself to the Bible all the time it has been readily available, and built upon all these ages of religious experience, we should be far along toward a better knowledge and experience of a good, full and peaceful life. A much better world would certainly have been the result. But too much dogmatism from ignorance (willful or otherwise) has fragmented every religious group in the world. We can truthfully say that we have not progressed very far from the worst of the Old Testament or, for that matter, from the worst of the New Testament found in the book of Revelation.

Jesus, the son of the carpenter of Nazareth, extracted from the Old Testament the Two Great Commandments and many of his teachings that show humankind a rational foundation for living as he lived. Had his followers of that day, and all those since, taken his "new commandment" (John 13:34) seriously, religious progress (an improving way of living) would have carried us far above spiritual achievements thus far attained.

Anyone can look at the homes of our own time and see why religious progress has been stunted. Religion is taught in the home either consciously or unconsciously. All the gods of wealth, security, power, ego, and social status have had their altars honored and celebrated with as great subtlety, or as flagrantly as any of the forms of pagan worship condemned in the Old Testament by the prophets of yore. Frequently, the Bible sits on the magazine stand or coffee table only to be dusted off before the preacher visits. It has become, for most, a useless symbol—certainly not a guide for teaching religion as a way of life.

If the true Christian religion—the Church invisible, i.e., all those past and present who uncompromisingly follow in the steps of Jesus—is to bring fulfilment for mankind, it will have to take full advantage of the human privilege to have and to know books and the Book. For it needs to discover all the errors of the past with all the blind alleys and to walk more surely in the love and with the love of our Father-Creator. The Church visible has too long been preoccupied with so-called "theology" and ritual and thus has missed the growth that comes with practice of Jesus' practical principles of love.

To sort out the visible Church from the invisible Church is in the dominion of the Father. Only He knows the inner minds of persons. Some hint may be found in just how genuinely at peace and happy an individual is or in how effectively a person meets a crisis or cares for all that the Creator has brought into being. But accurate judgment remains with the One who really knows.

If we are truly devoted to the will of our God-YAHWEH, we shall know well the Book He has kept secure for us in the literal translations and in the original languages. We shall make application of what we have learned there and then begin to build on that. So we shall leave those who follow us a bit more than was available to us at the beginning of our lifetime.

A good home founded on a loving family that lives like Jesus lived can soon make virtuous changes in the world around us. Such a home can make sure, gradual progress to fulfilment of the Two Great Commandments and Jesus' "new commandment". (John 13:34.)

Passing on the true religion is not difficult. It is all of the false religions that are difficult to explain. What cannot be easily explained to a child by word or deed is therefore obviously false. Love is taught by firmness and consistency. One can hardly teach a child respect for law if the child is told to watch out the rear window of a speeding automobile for any policemen. Of course, now-a-days they look ahead for radar. If we fail in trying to explain good reasons for our actions to a child, there is something wrong with those actions.

If you cannot understand a philosophical position, it is not necessary in getting to know the Father. If it is not possible to make an idea understandable to a little child, it cannot be a Christian idea. Jesus said: "...Let the children come to me. Do not hinder them, for theirs is the Kingdom of God." (Mark 10:14.)

I suspect that when people make the Christian religion difficult to understand, they are feeling around for excuses for their failure to give themselves completely to the will of the Father. It is just another form of rationalization justifying a willful or sinful nature. Complete is a very plain word. Not to understand it would require full intention or willful evasion.

# PART 4

## THE NATURE OF GOD

# Chapter 13

# On the Creator and Creation

It has been held that, if man should achieve the ability to create matter out of nothing, there would no longer be a need for God. But, with all the magnificent advances of science, there appears to be absolutely no signs on the horizon that such a possibility exists. Anyway, by nature, man still has to begin with something even to conceive the abstract idea of nothing. In this respect he is no more capable than the hearers of the second, the more primitive, story of creation found in Genesis chapter 2.

Even if it could be proven that out of nitrogen alone all that is can be created, someone (or thing) had to bring nitrogen into being. Whenever something is shown to be the cause of nitrogen's origin, it still would be a human necessity to find what brought that thing into being. So begins the philosopher's "infinite regress"—an impossible, intolerable human condition of the mind.. As the "Old Preacher" put it: "...He has given eternity into man's mind, yet in a way that he cannot find out what God has done from the first to the end." (Ecclesiastes 3:11.)

No great human discovery has bested the position of the people who gave us the first chapter of the Bible book of Genesis. They said simply: "To begin with, God..." (Literally in the Hebrew, "In beginning, God...") Science may hungrily continue to seek after how it all was done, but when mankind has gone as far as it can in the field of science, the "who did it and why?" will remain. At that point, science leaves off and religion alone must take over.

Man is a part of all that exists—a part of all that has been created. The first part of this statement is reasonably of science. The second part is of religion. For, if you say, "Man is created." you must also say someone did it. There the human mind is driven to the question, "Why?" which immediately follows on the question, "Who?" out of human necessity. Both of these questions indicate a natural curiosity (or hunger) in the human consciousness that itself reflects part of the nature of the Creator. He is found to be not just a super man but an infinite being reflected in the creature as an excellent artisan is reflected in his work.

Here, first of all, is an indication that the Creator wants man to seek after Him. The writers updating the materials in Numbers and Exodus in the reign of King Josiah wrote, "You are seeking YAHWEH your Strength and you have found Him for you are seeking Him with all your mind and with all your being." (Deuteronomy 4:29.)

Secondly, as these words indicate, those who respond to this hunger will be satisfied when (if) they use the highest part of their intellect to seek to know the answers to the questions "Who?" and "Why?" This promise is reinforced in one of the many meanings of His name YAHWEH: I [really] am being what I am being." So indicate the writers of Psalm 19, Psalm 139 and Genesis 1:27. That is to say that, in natural events, in the very nature of the human mind and in all reality, man's nature and existence tells him what his Creator is like.

The writer of Psalm 19:1-4 says:

> "The heavens are telling the glory of God
> and the firmament proclaims His handiwork.
> Day to day pours forth speech
> and night to night declares knowledge.
> There actually is no speech nor are there really
> words nor is a voice actually heard.
> Yet their message goes out into the earth,
> and what they are saying to the ends of the world."

So it is that he finds confidence in the order of the universe and in the world that reflects the reliability of the Creator's providence.

*On the Creator and Creation*

The writer of Psalm 8 (verses 3-6) cries out:

"When I look at thy heavens, the work of thy fingers,
the moon and the stars which thou hast established;
What is man that you call him to mind,
even the offspring of mankind that you are
looking after him?
Yet you cause him to be little less than God
and envelop him in glory and honor.
Causing him to have dominion over all the work of thy hands..."

The human creature is overwhelmed by the boundless nature of his own being—of his own mind. He is consequently struck by the magnificence of the One who made him so—for He must be very great to be able to create so marvelous a creature as the human being.

Psalm 139 carries this thought even further: (See verses 1-2 and 4.)

'Oh YAHWEH, thou hast searched me and you know—
You know when I sit and when I rise up;
You discern my thoughts from afar.
Even before a word is on my tongue
Oh YAHWEH, you know it completely."

Each one of us is perpetually and constantly wrapped in the full attention of the Creator. He did not bring us into being just to give us a start in the world and then abandon us so as to turn His attention to other matters—leaving us to fend for ourselves after bringing us forth—as is done to its young by the armadillo and certain other creatures.

YAHWEH keeps track of all that goes on in the minds of every one of us to the point where He is fully cognizant of every thought developing in each person's mind—before even it becomes fully formed so that he can put it into words. If we choose, He and we are constantly intimate. As true subjects and like our King, He is in us and we are in Him—The Creator and the creature, Parent and child.

# Chapter 14

# The Image of God

"So God created mankind in His own image, in the image of God He created him; male and female He created them." (Genesis 1:27.) So begins the Bible account of the nature of humanity. So also is the nature or personhood of YAHWEH revealed in His creature, adham or ho anthropos or mankind (using your preference of Hebrew, Greek or English.) Since infinite Spirit is not quite comprehensible (grasped) by those of us earth-bound in our thinking, we need to begin with a comparison or simile.

BOTH ARE SELF AND OTHER CONSCIOUS
　　In all religions, whatever god or gods are believed to exist, there is always a self and other consciousness that is likewise attributable to the object of worship. As among humans we think of "I" and "you", so it is naturally taken that the god or gods do likewise. No other way of thinking could possibly bring any meaning of relationship between the god and humans. The Bible is consistent in representing YAHWEH as self and other conscious. Look and see. Note especially the prophets.

BOTH ARE COMMUNICATIVE
　　Since there is a self and other consciousness in both man and God, so also this very factor requires communication between them. Just

*The Nature of God*

knowing that others exist raises questions. What is the other like? Since I think, what and how does the other think? Is the other friendly or adversarial? A meeting of the eyes deepens this curiosity. But Spirit does not have eyes! This physical experience with other creatures is first.

The perception of God or gods in other than human form comes very late in religious development. Once we leave the ancient mythologies, "image of God" takes on entirely different meanings. We learn from ages of experience that we dare not look to man to see what man is like. Humans are made in the image of their Creator.

When humans make a god or gods in their own image, horrible things are done in the name of religion. I suppose this makes mandatory some accurate perceptions of the Creator before humans can begin to know their own nature and purpose for existing. The wise "Old Preacher" concludes, "...reverence God and keep His commandments. All mankind exists for this purpose." (Ecclesiastes 12:13.) With all his frustrations and pessimism, the wise "Old Preacher" had gathered quite a few right and true views of the nature of both humans and the Creator.

BOTH ARE SOCIAL BEINGS

Since humans and their God are self and other conscious and communicative, they are both social beings. Communication brings into being fellowship. In good communication, we learn of our need for someone to share with and to do for—someone to spend ourselves on—someone to love. Note the first three chapters of Hosea and chapter 11. Please review relevant parts of part 3 - ON RELIGIOUS COMMUNICATION, page 35.

BOTH HAVE MORAL CHOICE

Love or lack of it produces knowledge of moral choice—freedom. Good common sense (that I consider to be inspiration or word of God) tells us that, if God is "good", He has to be able to be "bad". Similarly, if humans are good or bad, they have to be so by choice or they cannot be blamed for their actions. Any retribution, therefore, for that bad behavior would be unjust. If anyone loves, it must be by choice or it cannot be love.

The Muslim religion teaches that Allah makes men do good or evil and yet gives no credit for good behavior while punishing for evil. He has a right to do so because He is Allah. But this is to make God an unjust tyrant.

Such a god can never fit the word picture of His character found in Deuteronomy 34:6. His command to love Him in Deuteronomy 6:4 would be meaningless if He is not lovable . Further, He only sets up revealing consequences for loving or not loving. He does not in any way compel. Humans are left with freedom to choose even as YAHWEH is free to be what He is being.

As His name YAHWEH says it: "I will be being what I am being." We are like Him in this respect. We know this to be so because we feel guilty when we do wrong. Guilt is felt only when we have freely chosen to do what we believe to be a bad deed or have deliberately thought evil— or at least believe we have so chosen.

For humans, freedom of choice is not as absolute as for our Creator. He, being all powerful, had to relinquish a part of His omnipotence in order that we, His creatures, might have freedom of choice. But freedom of choice for humans is not necessarily to do. It is only to choose to do. (This is the "little less" of Psalm 8:5.) We may be frustrated in our choice of actions by lack of talent or opportunity. We may be prevented from doing what we choose by other humans or physical obstacles. A tone deaf individual or one having poor voice qualities can hardly become a great vocal musician. One poorly coordinated or lacking certain necessary body parts can hardly be a great athlete, where such is required. Many a martyr has been made when a deeply devoted person has sought to confront a well armed tyrant.

Fortunately, since our Father-Creator knows what we are thinking before we can put that thought into words, He knows the sincerity of our intent even if we cannot fulfill our desire. So with the malefactor who died on the cross beside Jesus: he had no opportunity to demonstrate the firmness of his acceptance of Jesus' way of life, but the Father knew how complete it was.

There is an over-all plan that the Creator has for His creation. That will be fulfilled. Our part in the fulfilment of that plan may or may not be fulfilled through us. It will be done in spite of us. His plan will be fulfilled, but we can choose to be or not to be a part of it. Our freedom to choose is unlimited, but we are limited in following through on many of the choices we make.

Our time on earth is limited, but what we would choose to do with that time is not limited. We have freedom of choice even if we do not have unlimited freedom to do all that we have chosen to do. Like our Father-Creator, we have freedom of choice, but the creature is a "little less" than the Creator.

## WE BOTH HAVE DOMINION

As Creator, we know that YAHWEH has dominion over His creation. By means of experience of the power to dominate all other creatures around him, man has learned of his own dominion. It is only when humans abuse their dominant role that things go wrong. When man tries to dominate man, he invades the Creator's dominion and generates evil. So we know that, like YAHWEH, we have dominion. But we must make allowance for areas of dominion that are not ours. Consequences teach us when we abuse or overstep the bounds of our dominion. (Consider wars, violent crime and repression as well as spoiling, waste and destruction of resources.) Nevertheless, like YAHWEH, we have dominion however limited.

## BOTH ARE CREATIVE

We know from the first verse of Genesis that YAHWEH is creative. We are like that too. Let a group of women plan a large meal, deciding upon one recipe. Each one will inevitably bring the same dish as planned, but each one will have the stamp of the individual preference on it. No two will be exactly alike. People working on an assembly line, on boring, repetitive tasks, always perform better if given an opportunity to make creative suggestions about their work. Every person needs a garden, art work, music as a hobby, or other such activity in order to be fulfilled. Our Father is creative and so are we.

## BOTH ARE SPIRIT

Our Creator is spirit. (See chapter 16, Spirit-What It Is-What It Does-How It Is Known.) That is to say: He transcends the physical. Only so can He occupy the same space as a human being. Only so, can He be

*The Image of God*

everywhere as the prophet Jeremiah says (23:23f.) Otherwise it would be ridiculous to believe, as many do, that all those who pray, wherever and at the same time, are certain to be heard.

How else can YAHWEH know what goes on in every human mind at all times, as the writer of Psalm 139:1-3 prophesied? What is remarkable here is that, if YAHWEH is Spirit, and we are made in His image—then we are spirit too. That being the case—we are not our body. We have a body.

We manifest ourselves in this world through our bodies by what we say and do. We are not physical, but we manifest ourselves through what we say and do physically with our bodies. Since Spirit has neither mouth nor ears—we do not need a mouth to speak to Him or ears to hear Him. Our communication with our Father-Creator is Mind-to-mind, Thought-to- thought.

We get an earthly glimpse of this kind of communication in the relationship of spouses, identical twins or very close friends who have come to know each other well enough to be able to perceive what the other is thinking before they make it known physically. As YAHWEH is Spirit, so we, His image, are spirit.

BOTH ARE IMMENSE

We know YAHWEH to be immense. He who created and sustains the universe must be greater than what He created. He is neither here nor there, but everywhere. He transcends space. We, being made in His image, can make the universe our object. We "comprehended" (held in our minds) earth before man returned from space with pictures of it. We are obviously greater than that which we can hold within ourselves. We too, then, transcend space.

Even now we can be pretty much where we are in our thoughts. Think of how much more this will be true when we are freed from the physical body. As Paul said about life after death (of the body): our body "is sown a physical body. It is raised a spiritual body" (soma pneumatikon, I Corinthians 15:44.) His problem is in communicating the idea of personhood or personality without the appropriate words. He does not know just how to say that we shall know and be known although the physical body is left behind.

## The Nature of God

When we note all those characteristics of the Person whom we know as YAHWEH, we realize that no body is needed to know person or personality. Spirit and spirit are persons. Our personhood is like that of the Father-Creator. We do not need a body to be known by or to know another. YAHWEH is a person and He is spirit. We are persons and we are spirit. We transcend space. We, like our Creator, are immense.

### BOTH TRANSCEND TIME

Even as we transcend space, so also we transcend time. The name YAHWEH tells us that our God is eternal—He always was and always will be. He says: "I will be being what I was being." As was noted in chapter 5, YAHWEH—The Sacred Name, the Hebrew imperfect verb form is timeless.

When Jesus says to the believing malefactor crucified beside him: "Amen, to you I say, today with me you shall be in the orchard (or park)." (Luke 23:43.) The Hebrew word pardas used here, rendered by the Greek paradeiso, refers to a park or preserve containing trees. The Greek translation of the Old Testament used paradeiso for the Garden of Eden. In any case, although death of their bodies is immanent, Jesus sees himself and the malefactor living on.

From the earliest of human burials discovered, we see evidence of a belief in an after-life. I shall deal with this more in chapter 23, Heaven and Hell. As image of the eternal Father—we are at least immortal. Our bodies die. We do not die! We are living for ever. We too transcend time.

### SUMMARY

These are the nine characteristics of the nature of our Creator known to believers. (Self and other consciousness, communicative, social, free or moral, having dominion, creative, spirit, immense and immortal. This last especially is an indication of the "little less".) Since we are made in the image of our Creator, we begin to know why we are like that.

But we sometimes tend to deny or abuse some of these qualities. The effects revealed in the history of mankind show us why we must look to the Father to see what we ought to be like if we wish life on earth to be good, rich, full and happy.

There is an integrity—a oneness with our given nature that brings an

*The Image of God*

inner peace. It gives us a feeling of completeness, or wholeness, which the Hebrews call shalom. The other word for it is at-one-ment. Jesus' prayer to the Father was, "The glory thou hast given me I have given to them, that they may be one even as we are one." (John 17:22.) The key means to that oneness is love. Remember the Two Great Commandments.

## REVIEW: THE NINE CHARACTERISTICS OF THE IMAGE OF GOD IN MAN

1. Self and other consciousness.
2. Comunicative.
3. Social or fellowship resulting from communication. We need an object to love--someone to share with and do for--to spend ourselves on.
4. Moral choice or freedom.
5. Dominion.
6. Creative.
7. Spirit: transcends the physical, but may be manifest through it.
8. Immortal, i.e., not limited by time. We are living forever whether we want to or not.
9. Immense, i.e., not limited by space. We can make the universe our object or comprehend it. We can take it within ourselves!

We dare not look at man to see what God is like. We must look at God to see what man is like or else we shall emphasize the wrong things. Even the things that are recorded about Jesus in our only source, the Bible, sometimes contradict and therefore must be tested against what we know of YAHWEH whom he worshipped and about whom he came to teach--and Jesus used nature (what God has done.)

# Chapter 15

# The Presence of God

Only Spirit can occupy the same space as a human being at the same time. As we learn what Spirit is, (See chapter 16 - Spirit—What It Is, What It Does, How It Is Known.) it becomes possible to acknowledge this opening statement. But how is one to know when or if Spirit is present?

First, one has to understand what Jesus meant when he said "God is spirit, and those worshipping Him must (it is necessary, dei) worship Him as (dative of means) spirit and truth." (John 4:24.) The nature of God's existence is as spirit. This is not new in the New Testament. In the second verse of the Old Testament this is acknowledged: "...and Spirit Power (or God weruhca eloheem) was hovering over the face of the waters." (Genesis 1:2.) YAHWEH is distinctly different from all that is physical.

Second, the Creator's presence in any living being is what is life to that being. As the poet says through Elihu: "If He (YAHWEH) should set His mind on Himself, He would gather to Himself His spirit, even His breath, and all flesh would expire at once, and man would return to dust." (Job 34:14f.) It is not a one time infusion of life in living beings, but a constant presence. If for a moment YAHWEH should withdraw His presence (attention?) from any living being, that one would cease to live. (See also Psalm 104:29f.)

So it is necessary that YAHWEH be infinite of being and everywhere present at all times. As the prophet Jeremiah reported: "'Am I a God nearby,' says YAHWEH, 'And not a God far off? Can a man hide himself in secret places and I not see him?' says YAHWEH. 'Do I not fill heaven and earth?'" (Jeremiah 23:23f.)

Since humans appear to be the only creatures fully moral, i.e., to have freedom of choice, there is more to the presence of God in them than in other creatures. Setting aside the aspect of the presence of Spirit as life, we note another side—at-one-ment. In Jesus' prayer in John 17, he prays for those who are persuaded by the gospel, "...that they may be one, even as you, Father, are in me and I in you, that they may be in us..." (verse 21.) Looking to Jesus' ministry and its climax in Gethsemane and the Cross, we find his atonement with YAHWEH to be complete obedience to the will of the Father—even to suffering and physical death where and when necessary.

Completely committed Jews as well as Christians have demonstrated this oneness down through the ages.

Holding to this aspect of Spirit and spirit, one can say that there is only one place where Spirit is not. Since only humans can refuse the will of the Father, this aspect of His presence we can refuse. In this regard, it can be said that the one place where YAHWEH is not is in the unrepentant person. God's attention is there, for the rebellious person still lives. (Physically speaking that is.) But, spiritually speaking, such a person is dead.

Jesus said: "...I came in order that they may have life, and have it abundantly." (John 10-:10.) Since the Creator is "a Mighty One, compassionate and gracious, patient, the very being of steadfast love and truth" (Exodus 34:6); since He is the loving Father-Creator—His will can only be for the richest and most satisfactory existence for each of His children (for every human being.) Not to accept YAHWEH'S will for our life therefore, does great injury to His love. To let Him in to guide our every thought and action would be for us the ultimate of heavenly existence here on earth. As Jesus would say: "living abundantly."

How are we to know when Spirit is present? Jesus clarified that once and for all in response to the lawyer's question, "...teacher, what shall I do to inherit eternal life?" and his statement of the Two Great

Commandments when Jesus asked the man to define the Law. "He (Jesus) said to him, 'You have answered rightly; this do and you shall live.'" (Luke 10:25-28.) That is to live truly in the spiritual sense—to experience the presence of God.

Since love is from God and, as the writer of the first Epistle of John says: "...God is love." (I John 4:8.) YAHWEH is the source. We are but the channel through which His love flows. When we are loving, we really know the presence of Spirit—YAHWEH. As the same writer said it: "No man has ever seen God; if we love one another, God lives in us and His love is completed in us." (I John 4:12.)

Love is the one thing of which it can be said: "The more you spend, the more you have to spend." Since the reservoir of love is YAHWEH, who is infinite love, the wider the channel, the more will flow. The more we allow to flow, the wider the channel becomes. You and I are the channels through which love flows when we allow Him to enter our person and so clothe Himself with us. It is in loving and being loved that we know the presence of Spirit-God.

# Chapter 16

# Spirit--
# What It Is,
# What It Does,
# How It Is Known

One might switch this topic and say: "Spirit Is what it Is and What it does, and That is how it is known." The word "spirit" springs in English from the Latin word spiritus meaning variously, "breathing, breath, gentle blowing of air, or a breeze." Its application to God originated long before science began to look to gas molecules of hydrogen and oxygen in motion as a definition of moving air.

YAHWEH was eventually conceived of as having no "form" or likeness. He is incomparable with any creature. (Deuteronomy 4:15ff.) So any attempt to portray Him by any physical means was "corruption" (shahcath) or sacrilegious.

The analogy of moving air, breath, or wind is appropriate. This generally is expressed in the Old Testament by the word ruhca, and in the New Testament by the word pneuma. Both refer to a power that cannot be seen although its effects are perceptible to the senses.

As the animating force in living creatures, its absence is seen in death. Wind is not seen, but the bough as it bends is visible. When, as the Bible says literally, the spirit "clothed itself with Saul", and he began to prophesy (I Samuel 10:6) and YAHWEH "...breathed into his nostrils the breath of life and there was man, a living being." (nephesh "soul" Genesis 2:7), God is seen to work in humans—to be in them.

By the time of the approaching captivity, Jeremiah could report YAHWEH as saying: "'Am I a God near by,' says YAHWEH, 'and not a God far off? Can a man hide himself in secret places and I not see him?' says YAHWEH. 'Do I not fill heaven and earth?'" (Jeremiah 23:23f.) The prophet Amos, about 150 years earlier, had expressed the same idea. (Amos 9:2-4.) Likewise the first two chapters of Jonah and the writer of Psalm 139:7-10 point our that there is no way one can get away from YAHWEH. The only way one could speak of such a God is by way of analogy—He is "spirit." For only such a being can be everywhere—eventually thought of as everywhere at once.

In our journey of thought to this point, we have not only come across some ideas of what spirit is, but also what Spirit (YAHWEH) is. He is as His name implies: infinite and everywhere present. Add more of Psalm 139 (verses 1-6 and 13-16) and we learn that He is all-knowing. We have seen throughout the Old Testament that there is no limit to His power. (The ubiquitous appearance of the word eloheem to identify Him—meaning Power or Might—is indicative of how He was perceived.)

Like the force of gravity, He is making known to us much of what He is by what he does. But this does not mean the we know Him entirely any more than we know gravity entirely. As the Old Preacher said: "...He has given eternity (golam) into their minds, yet so that mankind is not finding what God has done from beginning to end (rosh and soph respectively)." (Ecclesiastes 3:11.)

What Spirit does is seen in the story of creation. He has special concern for humans, making them a little less than Himself and granting them dominion. (Genesis 1:27f. and Psalm 8:5.) In clothing Himself with prophets, He is able to communicate by words to His human creatures. The expression, "the gift of God," is so much a part of our language because we recognize the intimate nature of our relationship with the Father. This expression covers superlative qualities that our training and genetic background cannot explain.

Great events in history reveal too many coincidences for coincidence to be a rational (even numerical—statistical) explanation. Recall the sudden plague on the Assyrians who were about to overwhelm Jerusalem (II Kings 19:35-37.) Consider also the failure of Hitler's forces to finish the job at Dunkirk and on "D" day when they had the means and opportunity. There are far too many coincidences involved in bringing into being a happy, enduring marriage of two people. It is no wonder that it is said, "A good marriage is made in heaven."

In the context of Psalm 104:29f., the providence, power and care of YAHWEH is praised: "When you hide your face [creatures] are dismayed; when you take away their breath they die and return to their dust. When you send forth your spirit, they are created and you renew the face of the ground." Spirit is what it does and so it is known. YAHWEH who is spirit, being infinite, is everywhere and yet is a person who knows all and has all power. Nevertheless He is compassionate, loving, patient, gracious and forgiving. (Exodus 34:6.)

Those who sometimes say that the Spirit is God in the Church from the time of Jesus have not read their Old Testament. As we see in the passages referred to above, the Spirit-God has been active in the Hebrew people and Church (synagogue and Temple) from the beginning. Spirit is not restricted by time or space or by the dogma or doctrine or creed of any sect. Spirit is God and God is Spirit. They are one and the same, not separate entities. Like Himself, He has made us spirit with all the boundless qualities of Spirit except for His eternal, ubiquitous and omnipotent qualities. Even then, He has made us but little less than Himself—boundless and immortal—creatures such as we are. We have a body. We are not a body. We too are spirit and indwelt by the infinite God!

# PART 5

## SIN AND ATONEMENT

# Chapter 17

# What Is Sin?

There are no less than six Hebrew words that refer to various forms of sin. The ideas range from missing the mark, going astray, stumbling and rebellion to mixing things that ought not to be mixed. In most cases, especially when referring to various "laws of Moses", such sin deals with failure to maintain proper ritual behavior as required in the first five books of the Bible. From the time of the ethical prophets, Isaiah, Hosea, Amos and Micah, the emphasis on freedom from sin is more on an inner loyalty and purity of mind toward YAHWEH and His will.

Micah summed up the basic requirements for a proper relationship with YAHWEH in 6:8: "He has shown you, O man (adham), what is good; and what does YAHWEH seek from you but to do justice and love steadfastness and to walk humbly with your God."

In the two previous verses, Micah rejects all ritual approaches even if they were to include the sacrifice of the first born. One can hardly think of a more costly sacrifice for the people of the Old Testament than to give the first born child. Such devotion is seldom found in modern religious adherents. Misguided though it was, it was the ultimate in an effort to be reconciled to YAHWEH or such other gods as were worshipped.

The more primitive religious atmosphere, out of which the Judaeo-Christian religions grew, saw man's role as a slave of the gods. In the Akkadian myth of the victory of Marduk over Tiamat, Marduk says to Ea: "...I will establish a savage, 'man' shall be his name...He shall be charged with the services of the gods that they might be at ease." (James B.

Pritchard, Ancient Near Eastern Texts, Princeton University Press, 1950, Page 68.)

In the Old Testament, the idea prevails in the many passages such as Genesis 8:21 where Noah had built an altar and began sacrificing burnt offerings of all clean birds and beasts, "And when YAHWEH was smelling the tranquilizing odor, YAHWEH said to Himself, 'I will never again curse the ground because of man...'" Thus the ritual of transferring gifts from earth to the gods was seen properly to be done by fire. So man, who made gods in his own image, sought to please or appease them.

It was not until the ethical prophets that sin was more clearly viewed as hurting the loving God YAHWEH. It was necessary for this understanding to blossom before the wrathful, vengeful conceptions of YAHWEH could be displaced. It was not until then that Exodus 34:6 could be fully accepted: "...'YAHWEH is YAHWEH, a God compassionate and gracious, patient and the very reality of steadfast love and truth.'"

Once this breakthrough is made, Jesus' number one main principle is possible: "Listen, O Israel, YAHWEH is our God. YAHWEH is one. So you shall love YAHWEH with all your mind and with all your soul and with all your strength." (Deuteronomy 6:4f.) It seems that Jesus coupled this with the second: "The stranger who dwells with you shall be as the native among you, and you shall love him as yourselves..." (Leviticus 19:34.)

At this point, we can see that sin is any lacking in love. This is true whether it be love of YAHWEH or love of any human or of His creation. Since YAHWEH as Creator is father of every human being, our experiences as parents and/or as children tell us clearly how destructive of the person is that lack of love wherever it may occur. Guilt for any other reason is misplaced and false. We shall deal with how to overcome true guilt in the following chapter 18 - Forgiveness-Atonement.

# Chapter 18

# Forgiveness--Atonement

The psalmist says: "Not according to our sin has He done to us, nor has He troubled us according to our guilt. For as the heavens are high above the earth, so great is His steadfast love upon those revering Him." (Psalm 103:10f.) People of the Old Testament used several words that referred to the forgiveness of offenses against YAHWEH: to cover over, to lift up or away, to pardon and to loosen or to send away. There are others less direct such as to restore, purify and to cleanse. The latter have more to do with ritual qualifications such as washing, sacrifice and redeeming or restitution.

The writer of Psalm 130:3f. says: "If YAHWEH was retaining guilts, Lord, who could stand? But with thee is forgiveness to the end that you may be revered." It may be seen that, far back in religious development, our spiritual forefathers knew something of grace—true forgiveness. There is no room here for penalty, payment, restitution or substitution.

As Abelard (11th and 12th century) put the question: "If a penalty is paid, where is the forgiveness?" For ever after, he left the religious mental gymnasts, who operate under the banner of orthodoxy, frustrated. They insist that, for there to be forgiveness by YAHWEH, Jesus had to pay the price of sin of people. But they have never been able to offer a simple explanation of how this involves forgiveness.

The Old Testament folk sought to appease an angry god by the shedding of blood—using some form of ritual offering, even to the sacrifice of the first born son. (Exodus 22:29.) This was modified in Numbers 3:12 where the Levites were to become a substitute.

Human sacrifice nevertheless persisted as can be seen in Judges 11:31ff., I Kings 16:34 and II Kings 23:10. Even down to the time of the "apostle" Paul, animals were slaughtered for such purposes (I Corinthians 8:7ff.) In fact, outside of Israel, the meat market was the pagan temple where the sacrifices were made. Old Testament sacrifices were made and utilized differently. The meat was burned and/or eaten by the priests or, in the case of peace offerings, eaten by the ones donating the animal along with the priests as a communion meal with YAHWEH. (Deuteronomy 27:6f.) YAHWEH'S portion was burned on the altar.

Where then is the forgiveness? Exodus 34:6 lays the groundwork for a knowledge of the gracious nature of YAHWEH'S love. The psalmist says: "Surely, a man cannot pay the ransom, or give God the price, (Hebrew capher "to cover over") for any ransom of his soul is precious and would be infinitely inadequate." (Psalm 49:7f.)

The very fact that one lives at all as a gift of YAHWEH makes it clear that no one has a thing that he can give. As another psalmist says for YAHWEH: "If I were hungry, I would not tell you, for the world and all that fills it is mine." (Psalm 50:12.)

Jesus told the parable of the father of the prodigal son. Upon the son's return to the father's care, the father runs to meet him. Not one word is said of repayment of a wasted heritage. Just the return, the repentance, the acceptance of the father's care, is all it takes. For the father who suffered the loss of the son, the wayward child is now no longer a cause of pain, but rather a cause of rejoicing. There is a complete change from hurt to happiness. That is forgiveness—atonement. (Note also the other parables in this 15th chapter of Luke, sometimes called the lost and found department of the Bible.)

Since the Father's desire for us is the absolute best, to do anything other than His will is injury to His careful love. That is why sin is bad. It is the only reason it is bad. That is why the very moment we return irrevocably to loving obedience to the will of YAHWEH, forgiveness has taken place.

It is redundant to ask for forgiveness. It is asking for something

*Forgiveness--Atonement*

already given out of gracious love—something that has already taken place. Such asking is near to sacrilege. The nearest that one can come to a proper request for forgiveness is in the feeling of sorrow for injury to that great love that leads to repentance.

The only possibility of unforgivable sin, therefore, has to be persistent and unchanging refusal to accept the will of our Father-Creator. As the prophet Jeremiah, speaking for YAHWEH, said: "Why then has this people turned away, Jerusalem turning away perpetually? They have held fast deceitfulness. They have refused to return." (Jeremiah 8:5.)

Also, the writer of the first Epistle of John writes: "...there is a sin to death. I do not say one is to pray concerning that." (I John 5:16.) To refuse to love and not to change, that is the only unforgivable sin—the "sin to death." Note that this comes from the one man who knew what Jesus meant by godly love (agape) contrasted with family love (philia). (John 21:15-19.)

To be one with the Father-Creator is to be fully in compliance with His will. How compliant? Note Jesus in Gethsemane that last night, and on the Roman cross. It is an individual—a personal matter. Nothing less than total—a Gethsemane type of commitment will do. Repentance from selfishness to love is the only means to forgiveness—atonement. No one can do that for us or on our behalf. Only the sinner can turn back from that sin. There is no other way to heal injured love.

# Chapter 19

# The Dogma of Substitutionary Atonement

Having spoken of forgiveness as free grace, one must face the dogma of substitutionary atonement. There is no satisfaction for the dogmatists in the question of Abelard. All they can do is ignore the common sense (inspiration) of the people who must insist that, if a price has to be paid, there is no forgiveness.

One can sympathize with the dogmatists' feeling of urgency for protection of the uniqueness of the role Jesus played in the religions of mankind. But such urgency is born of lack of faith in the power of truth. It is not necessary to give Jesus innumerable categories of uniqueness such as a miraculous birth, the power to perform miracles that over rule the order established by our Creator or bodily assumption after a time in the tomb. One may find, incidentally, matching miracles attributed to Elijah and Elisha in the mythologies created around them.

It is the life he lived in his three short years of ministry and his teaching by example that makes Jesus such a powerful influence in the world. Jesus said: "[I pray] that they may all be one even as thou, Father, art in me and I in thee, that they also may be in us...The glory which thou hast given me I have given to them that they may be one even as we are one, I in them thou in me, that they may be perfected into one, so that the world may know that thou hast sent me and hast loved them even as thou hast loved me." (John 17:21-23.)

He was constantly striving to show that whatever he could do and be, all humankind could and therefore should be and do. He speaks of himself again and again as only a human being, using the self-designating expression "son of man". The writer of the epistle to the Hebrews wrote: "In the days of his flesh, Jesus offered up prayers and supplication, with loud cries and tears to Him who was able to save him from death, and he was heard because of the reverence. Although being a son, he learned obedience through what he suffered; and being thus perfected he became the source of eternal salvation to all who obey him." (Hebrews 5:7-9.) The same writer reports: "For he who sanctifies and those who are sanctified have all one origin. That is why he is not ashamed to call them brethren." (Hebrews 2:11.)

The problem would be this: if Jesus were not in every respect as we are, we could always excuse ourselves from the obligation to be Christian (Christ-like). It would also make nonsense of Paul's references to the Church as the body of Christ.

We could always complain, "But I was not born of a virgin, therefore I am different." Or we could say that he had a special link with the Father as is seen in how he over rules the laws of creation, like the story of the slaying of the fig tree with a curse. (Mark 11:14 and 20.) Or we might use the story of Jesus walking on water (Matthew 14:25ff.)

But in the story of the slaying of the fig tree, Jesus concludes that anyone else could do as much or more if only they had confidence in God and did not doubt. (Mark 11:22f.) See also Matthew 14:28-30 and John 14:12.

Let us not forget the repentant malefactor who died on the cross beside Jesus. Of him Jesus said, "...Amen, to you I say, this day, with me, you shall be in paradise." (Luke 23:43.) Note the emphasis on "this day", and then, "with me". There is no time spent in cold storage awaiting a time when all humans, at the end of time, are gathered so that a judgment can be made on who is in and who is out, as though the Father-Creator could not make a fair decision before all mankind had lived, as in the book of Revelation 6:9-11 and chapter 20.

Love naturally would require restitution of material things in this life where possible, but there is no means what-so-ever of taking back an injury done to love. No one has anything with which to pay the Father for injury done to His love. No on can possibly do it for us. What the Father wants is our loving obedience to His will. He wants to give us the best life possible and that we may be the best for each other. No one can give this love for us.

Repentance—turning from hurting the Father and His people and His world to loving and caring for Him and His—is all that He desires of us. That alone is the means to "salvation" or happiness or paradise or heaven. If we don't have this in this life—we are likely never to have it in the life that follows death of the body. No one can achieve it for us.

As the psalmist put it: "He who brings thanksgiving as his sacrifice honors me; one who orders his way, I am causing to see the salvation of God." (Psalm 50:23.)

Why then did Jesus volunteer to die on the cross? That choice on his part removed the last excuse to which we might have resorted in avoiding a full commitment to obedience to the Two Great Commandments. Without Jesus' acceptance of his role in Gethsemane (Mark 14:36) and his follow-through to the Cross, humankind would still be asking, "What must I do to inherit eternal life?" (Mark 10:17.)

Or we might be asking, "What does it mean to love YAHWEH with all my mind, soul and being?" Since the Cross, there is no longer any excuse from total commitment or from knowing what it means.

No one, not even Jesus, could repent for us. Each individual has to make that choice for himself. That is the sole requirement for "salvation"—the sole means to heaven here or hereafter. Jesus died on account of human sinfulness, not for our sin. The Greek translates equally well this way. Dogmatism has led to the latter translation in spite of its incompatibility with good common sense.

If one cannot be like Jesus, he is doomed. There are no excuses. As Jesus said: "A new commandment I give you, that you love one another even as I have loved you..." (John 13:34.) That love carried Jesus, and the malefactor dying with him, directly to "Paradise" the same moment their bodies died on the cross. No one finds "Paradise" in any other way. Nothing else is required.

# Chapter 20

# Satan, That Old Devil, the Serpent

If ever we take time to sit down and think, instead of drifting along in a bubble of habit, haste, or lethargy, we marvel (May even be shocked) at what we discover in our minds—especially the contradictions we find there. Some of the most confused thinking (aside from that on the nature of God) is in the realm of sin and the "devil". This confusion continues as long as we carelessly substitute myth for reality.

The story of the Garden of Eden (Genesis Chapter 3) and mankind's (adam's) first encounter with the "wise old serpent", is a mythological way of getting across a profound idea that man can be led astray by his own desires or curiosity. I.e., he can be led astray—if he wants to be!

In the Old Testament, the serpent character appears in only this passage and two others. The latter two are obviously poetic references to "Tiamat", mother of all the gods in the Babylonian mythology. (Job 26:13 and Isaiah 27:1.)

Satan appears only briefly in the Old Testament. In I Chronicles 21:1 he is the one who causes David to number the people of Israel contrary to the will of YAHWEH. Compare the earlier version of the story in II Samuel 24:1 where it says that YAHWEH moved David against the people. In both cases, the writers say that this is because YAHWEH was angry with the people and sought an occasion to lower the boom on them.

The discrepancy between the two accounts is easily understood when one realizes that Chronicles was written in Babylon by the people who had been influenced by Zoroastrianism there. They appear to have decided to use this means of taking the burden off YAHWEH as they falsely perceived Him. It is a small movement (even if in the wrong direction) toward the maturer view of the writer of the epistle of James (1:13): "Let no one say, when he is tempted, 'I am tempted by God'; for God cannot be tempted with evil and He Himself tempts no one."

Another passage to be considered is in Zechariah 3:1-2. In his vision, Zechariah sees Joshua in court before YAHWEH with Satan (or the adversary, the actual meaning of the Hebrew word satan.) It is part of the vision in which Zechariah sees Joshua in need of being purged of his sin so that he may become the High Priest of the post captivity temple.

Zechariah, back from Babylon, also has picked up a bit of Zoroastrianism or else the translators inconsistently (for doctrinal reasons) transliterate the word here instead of translating it as elsewhere. In using the Hebrew word with capitalization, they make it a means of personifying the power of evil.

A third appearance of "Satan" is that incompatible portion of Job (Chapters 1 and 2) added by someone bent upon destroying the effectiveness of the poem. Here, as in Chronicles and Zechariah, Satan appears and then disappears as quickly. From Job 2:7 on, Satan is never mentioned again until one gets to the apocrypha and pseudepigrapha and questionable passages in the New Testament. Belief in a personal Satan is neither Hebrew nor Christian—it is Zoroastrian.

The Devil (Greek diabolos, "slanderer") occurs only in the New Testament, not at all in the Old Testament. Between the testaments, these three figures were merged with the Greek philosophies and demonology by writers among the Pharisees, who gave us most of the literature of that period with such wild visions as are found in Revelation 12:7-9.

Except for Paul and Luke and the writer of the epistle of James, the New Testament writers were very poorly educated. Imaginative works always attract such folk. Paul was also a Pharisee. He, with Luke, would have been steeped in the neoplatonic demonology of that day.

Although these facts have been before us for generations, there are still many people who like to believe that their evil impulses are authored by some such person-like power. From Genesis they find the "serpent" who is the tempter. "Satan" as the adversary or opposer of God comes later. Then they find the "Devil" as the slanderer of God and of others.

However, in no place in the Bible is this three-faceted character given the role of assuming man's responsibility for his sin! As Ezekiel well summarized it: "The soul that sins shall die. The son shall not suffer for the iniquity of the father, not the father for the iniquity of the son. The righteousness of the righteous shall be upon himself, and the wickedness of the wicked shall be upon himself." (Ezekiel 18:20.)

There is no one we can blame for the way we choose to act. Otherwise, we would have no reason to feel guilt. There is an individual responsibility for sin because we are responsible (able to respond). A just God blames no one for what he cannot help being or doing.

What then, is the value of these three figures in a moral religion? They point out three characteristics of sinful behavior: (1) When we tempt others, we are the "Serpent", whether we do so by provocative acts or by what we teach. (2) When we oppose the will of the Father-Creator, whether by default or by willful acts, we are the "Satan". (3) When we slander YAHWEH or our neighbor, whether by words or deeds, we are the "Devil".

Shakespeare said that all the world is a stage and we but actors in it. We play the role we choose. We can be Serpent, Satan, or Devil. But, if we choose to live—really live fully and joyfully and gratefully—then we have chosen the role YAHWEH has given to us. If we take the role of Jesus and live his part, there will be no need to look for someone upon whom to shift the blame.

Sin is willful disobedience. No one makes us do wrong. If they did, they would be the ones to blame. There is a Serpent, a Devil and a Satan. But, like Santa Claus to our children, it is you or me. We ought not to burden the mythical Satan, the poor old Devil or the Snake with the blame that we ourselves should be carrying.

We are able to respond to the will of the Father-Creator in all things according to His will. That is why we feel guilty when we do wrong. That is why we are said to be responsible.

# PART 6

## LIFE, DEATH AND AFTER

# Chapter 21

# Life and Death in the Bible

Although the Old Testament reveals a general view of "death" as being the cessation of life in the usual sense, it deals with death in living more. In the New Testament, for the most part, one sees life as a continuation of self and other consciousness that prevails even after death of the body similar to that flashing glimpse in Job 19:26f. This makes death only an interlude experience between death of the body and that which follows, whether physical or spiritual.

A short scientific definition of life is that state of an individual animal or plant in which its organs are capable of performing their functions. From this point of view it is possible for a person to have too much "life" in some parts and not enough in others. Take for example cancer and severe allergies.

Another scientific definition of life is that property of plants and animals which makes it possible for them to take in food, change it to energy, grow, adapt and reproduce. But each healthy cell in the human body fulfills all those conditions, even in a brain dead person.

Science still puzzles over human life. When does it begin? When does it end? Does one evaluate it by consciousness or by organic signs or both? How do mind and brain figure in such an evaluation? At this point, we come very close to leaving the realm of science and move into the sphere of religion. Psychology (soul study) is the in-between territory—hardly science and almost religion.

Genesis 1:30 defines as living that creature that has the soul of life (nephesh hcayah) in it. In the more primitive account of creation (Genesis 2:7) it says, "Then YAHWEH God...is blowing into [man's] nostrils the breath (nishmath) of lives (hcayah plural) and there was mankind (haadham) a soul of life (or "living being" by transposing these two words.)"

One who has breath or has not bled to death is alive. One who has "expired" or whose blood has been poured out is dead. As it is written in Leviticus 17:14, "For the soul (life? nephesh) of all flesh (basar) is in the blood..." (See also Deuteronomy 12:23.)

The Old Testament word for soul (nephesh) generally refers to the living essence of a living being—the animating factor of that which lives. The Hebrew word ruhca (e.g., Genesis 6:3) sometimes carries the same meaning. But only the context clarifies how these words are being used. Therefore, one must be especially careful in dealing with their translation.

The Hebrews counted death as total annihilation. This is to be seen in passages like II Samuel 14:14 where the wise woman of Tekoa says: "For we are certainly dying and are like water being poured out on the ground which cannot be gathered up." (Note also Job 14:7-19.)
It is natural then that they would consider the quality of life all important just so long as it was a natural or normal span of years: "There are seventy years in our life span, if with strength, eighty years..." (Psalm 90:10.) That was a blessing. More was not considered.

Anything short of a good full life or a normal span then, is a degree of death. Ezekiel (37:11) recounts the laments of his people in exile, reading the message from the valley of dry bones: "Then he said to me, 'Son of man, these bones represent the whole house of Israel. Behold, they are saying dried up are our bones and perished is our hope. We are cut off.'" We see the psalmist lamenting failure in battle: "On account of thee we have been slain all the day, considered as sheep for slaughter." (Psalm 44:22.)

Job, suffering from all his ailments and material losses, cries out: "My soul is destroyed, my days are extinguished, the grave is for me!" (Job 17:1.) He is very much alive here as we can see from how well he holds up his part of the dialogue. All kinds of unhappy situations incite the composers of the various psalms to cry out in one way or another, "We are dead!" (See another effective example in Psalm 143:3-7.)

With the dominant view in the Old Testament being total annihilation, it is no wonder that there are so many protests and complaints offered to the all-powerful Creator-Sustainer for illness, misfortunes, poverty and oppression.

The writer of Psalm 103 says: "A human, his days are like grass, like a flower of the field he blooms; for the wind (ruhca) passes over him and he is gone and his place does not recognize him any more." (Verses 15f.)

YAHWEH lives for ever. In comparison, this makes even a full human life span seem very short—only a breath, or as the Old Preacher said it: "For who knows what is good for human life from the number of days of his futile life that he passes like a shadow?..." (Ecclesiastes 6:12.) What is to be found in life is all in the present and death ends all that completely for an individual.

The position of freedom of choice taken in Deuteronomy 30:19f. is rare in the Old Testament. Like much of the book of Job, the Old Testament gives YAHWEH arbitrary powers that often overshadow the gift of freedom of choice. Note particularly the account of Pharaoh in Exodus 9:12ff. and Deuteronomy 13:1-5. At times, it is more Muslim than Hebrew.

Muslim "Kismet" partly refers to the belief that Allah makes one do good or evil. Yet He gives no praise or blessing for doing good, but can punish for doing evil simply because He is God.

The Hebrew at least emphasizes blessings for good behavior and penalty for bad. Mixed in here and there (Hosea, for example, especially chapter 11) is forgiveness and covenant that mitigates just penalty incurred by wayward Israel or individuals. Old Testament ideas are ambivalent to say the least.

Jesus put a new and different perspective on both life and death. Nearly everywhere in the Bible, we are taught that life is a gift of our Father-Creator. It is sustained by Him. It can be a blessing or a curse. Jesus emphasized the fact that we alone determine which it shall be. If we want life to be a blessing, no matter what the circumstances, it will be a blessing.

## Life, Death and After

He often taught from the book of Deuteronomy. There (30:19) Moses is reported as saying: "I cause heaven and earth to testify to you this day; I set life and death before you, blessing and curse. So choose life that you may live, you and your descendants." Which we shall choose is up to us.

Jesus said: "...I came in order that they might have life and have it luxuriously." (John 10:10.) Out of Deuteronomy and in its application to daily life he gave the method of precisely how to achieve that luxurious life. It is by love, loyalty and faithfulness toward our Father that life is blessed. He set up the first part of the Shemag (Deuteronomy 6:4f.) as the main requirement for the good and full life.

Jesus said that the first of all the commandments is: "...Listen Israel, YAHWEH is our God, YAHWEH is one, and you shall love YAHWEH your God with your whole heart and with your entire strength." (Mark 12:30.) Deuteronomy 30:20 adds a different but similar touch: "Love YAHWEH thy God heeding His voice, clinging to Him for that is your life and length of days..."

In another place, Mark reports Jesus as saying that any lack of full commitment deprives one of eternal life. For although a rich man (Mark 10:17ff.) had kept all the Ten Commandments, he still appeared to love wealth more than he did YAHWEH and therefore failed in his desire for eternal life.

In Luke 10:25-28, Jesus is reported to answer another about the qualifications for eternal life. When that one recites the Two Great Commandments, Jesus simply says:..."This do and you shall live." (verse 28.) The one and only criterion for life that is good and full and that does not end with death of the body is therefore to love God and man. To love, one must be free.

Those who love know the good life. Since life, from Jesus' point of view, does not end with death of the body, death takes on a very different meaning from that of the Old Testament. The Sadducees and Pharisees, still earth-bound in their thinking (Mark 12:18-27), could not understand eternal life. They could not understand Jesus' use of the words life and death either.

As I wrote in chapter 23, we choose the state in which we are living. One state is where love is lacking—a kind of vacuum. That is "hell".

Heaven, Jesus refers to as life. Hell is properly, then, the opposite or death. In some respects, the Old Testament folk caught the vision. Anything less than a good, full life is a degree of death.

At some time in this earthly existence, according to Jesus' point of view, we must choose between the two. That choice is arbitrary, complete and irrevocable. Death of the body is the absolute dividing line.

But it would be unfortunate indeed if one continues in any degree of death when life in all its fullness and goodness is freely available to all—the "luxurious" life offered by Jesus of Nazareth. (John 10:10.)

We are living forever whether we want to or not. We are free to choose how we shall live now and ever after. It is not how long we live on earth that is important. Look at Methuselah. He is said to have lived longer than any other man. What a pity that all that can be said of him is that he lived so long!

By contrast, look to Jesus of Nazareth. In three short years of his ministry—three short years of his life—he changed the whole world for good so that it can never be the same again. His total life span was hardly more than thirty years. His work as an itinerant teacher lasted only about three years, just one tenth of his life. Yet he gave all humanity the way and the truth and the life by which really to live.

Life in the Bible is not limited to any scientific definition. It is a gift of the Creator-Father. It is sustained by Him. It can be a blessing (life) or a curse (death). We alone determine which. As Jesus said: "...I came in order that they might have life and have it luxuriously." (John 10:10.)

And how did he say this luxurious life is to be achieved? He says, "If you keep my commandments you will rest in my love, even as I have kept my Father's commandments and rest in His love. These things I have spoken to you in order that my joy may be in you and that your joy may be filled." (John 15:10f.)

Death of the body is no more nor less than the shucking of an instrument in which we are being prepared for life as true spirit. In some ways it may be likened to a cocoon of a beautiful butterfly. And who cares for the cocoon after the butterfly has flown except for those practical uses that may be a help to bodies still living.

# Chapter 22

# "Salvation" in the Bible

There is both a secular and a religious definition for the word "salvation" and you will find both of these usages in the Bible. Generally, however, the Old Testament makes no such distinction between secular and sacred. In the New Century Dictionary and in the Webster's New World Dictionary one finds that the English word comes from the Latin salvare. Variously, our word is used as the act of saving or the state of being saved or delivered. "In theology," the New Century Dictionary defines it as "saved from the power and penalty of sin." Webster's has: "3. In theology, spiritual rescue from sin and death; saving the soul through the atonement of Jesus; redemption." Both of these are taken from Christian doctrine based on parts of the New Testament.

From beginning to end, "salvation" in the Old Testament refers to being saved from illness, poverty, or an early death or from oppression by others as an individual, a family, or a nation. In Genesis 48:16, Jacob speaks of being redeemed (gaal) from all the trials he has had to face in his long lifetime. In Exodus 6:6, YAHWEH promises to deliver (natsal) Israel from slavery in Egypt even to redeem (gaal) them with great power.

In Hosea 13:14, the prophet refers to redeeming (padhah) from sheol or redeeming (gaal) from death—here a synonymous parallel. Both lines of the poem are speaking of saving from death (untimely, of course). As Job generalizes: "So man (gebher) dies and is prostrate. A human

105

(adham) expires and is no more." (Job 14:10.) Note also Ecclesiastes 3:19f.

David refers to being redeemed (padhah) from trying circumstances throughout his life. A different word yet is found in the Hebrew of Psalm 136:24 in reference to being saved or "snatched away" (paraq) from their enemies.

Another approach to speaking of being saved makes use of the Hebrew verb form that means to cause a thing to happen. In Joshua 6:25, because Rahab has saved the spies, it is said, "Joshua caused her to live (Hiphil hcayah). The same usage is found in the story of Joseph's administration in Egypt. The people say, "You have caused us to live..." (Genesis 47:25.)

Another frequently used word in the Old Testament (yashag) means to liberate, make wide, and in the causative forms, speaks of being saved or delivered. In Exodus 14:30 it is written: "YAHWEH saved Israel that day from the hand of the Egyptians..." as Israel escaped across the Reed Sea. This is the most used Hebrew word for "salvation".

You will note that, in the Old Testament, "salvation" always refers to practical and immediate matters. This is so, as noted above, for Old Testament people speak of being saved from illness, early death, poverty, oppression and exile, even from anxiety, as they address YAHWEH.

When we arrive at the New Testament, however, we are in a completely different atmosphere. It is true that references in the Old Testament are made to saving (hcalats) one's soul (nephesh) as in Psalm 6:4. But this too is only because the petitioner wishes that YAHWEH will keep him around in the world that he may continue to give the halleluyah.

But in the New Testament, to be saved always refers to the dictionary meaning as given "in theology". So it can be seen that the words redeemed, ransomed and saved are literally synonymous in the New Testament as in most cases in the Old Testament. But the New Testament has a very different reference.

The Old Testament always refers to a current state of the individual, family or nation. This is true because death is thought of as complete annihilation or cessation of existence of the individual. Spirit (ruhca) or soul (nephesh) or breath (neshamah) are only signs of life. Absence of any of these or of blood (dam) is death. Hence the Hebrew onomotopoetic word to expire (gawag), the sound of the "death rattle" as it used to be called as one breathes out his last breath.

In the time between the Old Testament and the New Testament history, i.e., between the time of Alexander the Great and the beginning of Jesus' ministry, the infusion and absorption of Greek philosophies opened the way for Hebrews to look upon life as continuing beyond death of the body.

It was the Greeks who taught the separate distinctions between body, soul and spirit. However, as we see in Paul (I Corinthians 15), Christians, for the most part, reunited soul and spirit. Jesus' words to the malefactor who died with him on the cross laid the foundation for Paul's thoughts on a spiritual "body" (or identity) in the life of one whose physical body had died. Those of us who have crossed the line know of it.

Since the poet who gave us the book of Job showed so clearly that justice is not completed in this physical life, it is necessary that persons continue to live and render an accounting in the life after the body dies. This judgment on the way one has lived on earth is the focus of the New Testament when the word "salvation" is being considered.

Matthew 22:1-14 records Jesus telling a parable of a king giving a wedding feast on behalf of his son. First the regular list of guests is invited. When they fail to come, everyone reachable is invited. One of these comes in informal dress and, with those on the original list, is condemned. Luke, in his earlier interpretation of the parable (Luke 14:15-24), only has those invited who fail to come condemned.

In both accounts, the call is issued to all. This makes the offer of salvation freely given to all. Matthew records a concluding statement of Jesus: "For many are called but few are selected." (Matthew 22:14.)

This appears too partial of Jesus—the kind of thinking that led to the dogma of arbitrary election hinted at by Calvin but brought to its fatalistic conclusion in the Synod of Dort. However, in both gospel accounts of this parable, Matthew's concluding sentence (22:14) would be out of place according to the context. We go more deeply into related ideas in the chapter 23 and in part 10, chapter 34, Heaven Here and Now.

The New Testament read carelessly has produced creeds and dogmas on both sides of freedom of choice versus arbitrary election for

*Life, Death and After*

salvation or damnation. Common sense (inspiration) tells us that there are grounds for guilt only if we are responsible (able to respond.) It is not difficult to determine which side of the contradiction is the word of God here.

Salvation may be likened to a person walking on a wall (this earthly life.) One side is dark and lonely. The other side is bright, lovely and warm with good company. All walk the wall and must choose one side or the other before reaching the end (death of the body.) The wall ends in the outer darkness where people weep and gnash their teeth. (Matthew 22:13.)

YAHWEH'S invitation is like that issued by Joshua: "If it is wrong in your eyes to serve YAHWEH, choose this day whom you will serve..." (Joshua 24:15.) In the New Testament the choice is once and for all time, for both this life and that following death of the body. The call to choose is issued to all of mankind.

While walking the wall between the two choices, we only half live. It is not possible to live on both sides, for each is the opposite of the other. As the First Epistle of John puts it: "There is no fear in love, but perfect (teleia) love casts out fear..." (I John 4:18.) Fear, i.e., anxiety or worry, always exists where one has not decided which side of the wall to choose.

Selfishness (possibly rebelliousness) is the original and universal sin. That comes with freedom of choice. Like a splinter felt but ignored in the heat of intensive activity, failure to make this mandatory choice between the two ways undermines one's peace of mind. This is so even if he has not had the choice plainly presented. If he is informed of the necessity of choosing and still does not decide, it is devastating to his equilibrium.

Here is the root of human motivation to religion—an uneasiness—a hunger manifested by humans since our first evidence of mankind's thought. This plain presentation of both the nature of the choice and the urgency to "get off the wall" was the whole purpose of the life of Jesus. He said: "No servant can serve two masters. You cannot serve God and wealth." (Luke 16:13.)

When Jesus said, "Peace I leave with you, my peace I give to you, not as the world gives I give you..." (John 14:27), he was referring to "salvation" that alone is brought by absolute commitment to the will of

## "Salvation" in the Bible

the Father-Creator that he exemplified in his entire ministry. For only in that unequivocal decision for the right side of the "wall" can the tension be removed. That new state of peace is "salvation", what it means to be saved.

To be saved is to live as the Father intended—fully, joyously, wholesomely—inwardly at peace. It has nothing to do with the boring, frustrating, lustful, fearful, anxious, jealous, confused life of the unconverted or unreborn.

Nicodemus was a man whose sincerity and devotion could not be questioned. He was a Pharisee and on the ruling body of Israel. But he was not satisfied with the world standard of purity of his party. Generally, the Pharisees felt that they had achieved purity already. At great risk to his high standing in the community, he came to Jesus at night. He wanted the greater purity that he knew he lacked. He felt that Jesus could help him find it. When Jesus said, "Amen! Amen! I say if one is not born all over again he is not able to see the Kingdom of God." (John 3:3), Jesus had to go on struggling to lift Nicodemus' mind from the physical-bound Pharisee perspective to make him understand.

In his remarkable letter from prison to the Philippians, Paul reveals the peace that has come to him in having given himself over entirely to the will of God no matter what the cost. He says: "Rejoice in the Lord always. Again I say rejoice!" (Philippians 4:4.) He adds in verses 6f., "do not be anxious...but in all things with prayer and petition with thanksgiving, your requests make known to God and the peace of God which surpasses all understanding will keep (or guard phroureo) your hearts and minds in Christ Jesus."

"Salvation" in the Old Testament is limited to this earthly life. In the New Testament, the look is to the future life after death of the body. Many different ideas float about in the visible Christian Church as well as in modern Judaism regarding what life after death of the body will be like, or whether there shall be one at all.

But one thing most agree upon is that salvation is (from the time the Greek philosophies were absorbed) applied to the life that follows death of the body. Some of these will hold that this life of peace may begin before—i.e., when one is converted to the will of the Father-Creator. I know and share this peace with many friends.

*Life, Death and After*

It is my conviction that all of us will find out soon enough. We shall find that no one really dies. I am certain that many will be surprised at who is present and who is absent from the fellowship on the right side of the "wall". I believe that we are living forever whether we want to or not. Our choice is only how we shall live now and after death of the body. That choice must be made in this life. There will never be another chance.

When does come one's last chance to choose? Only God knows as Jesus said: "Concerning that day or the hour, no one knows...except the Father." (Mark 13:32.) If one is ready now, it will make no difference when it comes to him. To fret and be anxious about salvation is wrong.

One should not be fleeing from hell. Rather, the one who is running to the Father in response to His love is always at peace—already has the peace that surpasses understanding—already knows "salvation".

# Chapter 23

# Heaven and Hell

Job cries out: "Who gives that thou wouldst hide me in sheol...that thou wouldst appoint a set time, then remember me...All the days of my service I would wait till my release should come." (Job 14:13f.) If only there was a hope that he might live again, all his suffering would be tolerable. By the 19th chapter, the poet is ready to say that it has to be so: "So, after my skin has been thus destroyed, then without my flesh I shall perceive God, whom I shall see for myself, and my eyes shall behold and not another's." (Verses 26 and 27)

The poet recognizes that any kind of existence after death has to be self and other conscious or it has no meaning. This is just a spark of insight by which the poet tries to push back for a moment the overwhelming teaching of the Old Testament tradition that death is total annihilation.

As the wise woman of Tekoa put it: "We must all die, we are like water spilt on the ground which cannot be gathered up again..." (II Samuel 14:14. See also Job 14:7-12 and 18ff.) And as the psalmist says: "When his (man's) spirit departs he returns to the earth. On that very day his thoughts perish." (Psalm 146:4.)

It is only for the moment that the pressure of the crushing burden of the accusations of his three friends—and the injustice of it all—that Job is given this insight. The thought is soon swallowed up again in the

*Life, Death and After*

pervading idea of personal annihilation at death.

The poet rebels against the teaching that those right with YAHWEH will have health, wealth and long life, while those at odds with His will experience the opposite. All justice is meted out in this life. Rewards and penalties are completed either in each person's life or are passed on to his descendants.

The poet argues against the "justice" of the latter idea: "You say, God stores up his (the guilty one's) wickedness for his sons. Let him (God) put the penalty to him (the guilty one) so he is knowing it." "For what delight has he in his household after him?" (Job 21:19 and 21.) This is also borne out in Hezekiah's response to his reprieve from the penalty due him for showing all his wealth to emissaries of Babylon. (II Kings 20:12ff.)

The injustice in the world in that the wicked prosper while the good suffer is emotionally stated by Job, as the mouthpiece of the poet, especially in chapter 21. He concludes: "Have you not asked those who travel the roads, and do you not accept their assurances that the wicked is spared in the day of oppression, that he is spared in the passover? Who declares his way to his face? Who requites him for what he has done when he is borne to the grave?..." (Job 21:29-32.)

Although there is no belief in an afterlife in the Old Testament, aside from this brief glimpse in the book of Job, many subtle influences inevitably produce fruit in the times of the Apocrypha and Pseudepigrapha (which includes the last six chapters of Daniel) that climax in the teachings of Jesus in the New Testament.

It was necessary that the spiritual leaders of the Hebrews avoided thoughts on an afterlife because of pagan forms of worship attached to such beliefs. But as religious thought matured to the idea of humans being made in the image of their creator who had all the infinite characteristics summed up in the name YAHWEH, belief in a fully conscious life following death of the body was inevitable.

Along with the belief in an afterlife, however, must come an expectation of the fulfilment of justice in that time following death. This is the sole basis for any morality—the only alternative to brute dominance and exploitation among humans. It raises a sense of right-wrong, truth-falsehood, good-bad, fair-unfair in this life on earth.

## Heaven and Hell

Since humans are not governed by instincts, (or at least, since they are able to overrule them in some respects) the world would be a chaotic place indeed if mankind did not recognize the need for social controls. The cause effect experience of primitive humans, as they began to live in larger and larger groups, produced the rudiments of what we have in the last six of the Ten Commandments.

But men still lorded it over one another. In some respects—like the beasts around them—rule went to the strong.

With the development of fire and weapons for a better means of survival, time to use their higher potential for thought brought about an evaluation of their relationships to each other and to the world around them. Thus began the consideration of right and wrong and questions about origins and a search for explanations of the mysteries of their environment.

Social controls require penalties for violations. We can see how a sense of justice would be present in the minds of members of a primitive society since our children reveal a strong perception of justice at a very early age. So, with the poet who gave us the book of Job, we can see that there are many cases when there truly is no justice in this life. Therefore it must be meted out after death of the body to knowing persons or it is not justice.

Obviously, there are two choices available to humans. In this life, as well as after, the choices remain the same. Those who carefully and honestly examine themselves recognize that (aside from chemical aberrations in an individual) each of us has full control over whether we shall be good or bad, happy or unhappy. The mind of a person—his personhood or soul is his to turn in either direction he chooses.

Heaven and hell are states of being. They are not places. Fear may deprive one of his rational faculties. But fear is not a mandatory experience. As the writer of the First Epistle of John said it: "There is no fear in love, but mature love casts out fear..." (I John 4:18.)

So there are two states of being for us to choose from: (1) To be loving. (2) Not to be loving. Here again, common sense will verify the truth of this statement if we look at ourselves when we are loving and when we are not. To fulfill the Two Great Commandments is to enter the state of heaven. Those times when we are not at one with these commandments are certainly our genuine experience of hell.

Jesus uses two figures of hell. On the one hand he says: "...the sons of the kingdom (of the world) will be thrown into outer darkness where there will be weeping and gnashing of teeth." (Matthew 8:12.) In Mark 9:47f. he says the condemned will be "...thrown into the place of weeping where their worm does not die and their fire is not quenched."

The Greek word here is a rendering of the Hebrew ge hinnom valley of weeping, that refers to the place outside Jerusalem where Molech worship was practiced in times past. A large iron statue of the fire god stood there. Its arms formed a cradle for infants being sacrificed. They were placed in the statue's arms heated white hot by a great fire. Naturally, parents would weep at the sacrifice. Hence the name.

Subsequently, the place was desecrated by making it the city dump where, among other things, corpses of foreigners and dead beasts were cast. The dump fires smouldered continuously. The figure in Mark 9:47f. aptly describes this dump.

It was clear that Jesus was using a figure since fire and darkness are incompatible. It is appropriate, however, in that it portrays the ultimate worst that can happen to a person. Physical pain is limited for us in that pain beyond physical endurance causes one to lose consciousness.

Psychological pain, on the other hand, is not limited. Since one is freed of the body at death, we are speaking of the ultimate worst in what we call hell. Can we conceive of anything worse than to be perpetually isolated in a fully self and other conscious state.

Since all communication in life after death of the body is mind to mind as it is now between us and our God; and since all that we think is then immediately available to others; is it any wonder that those who have not purged their minds of all unlovely thoughts cannot be permitted in the company of heaven after this life on earth?

We need to keep in mind here that no one sends us to hell—or to heaven for that matter. We choose the state in which we are existing and shall exist.

To ask, "Where is hell?" is much like asking, "Where is heaven?" The answer to the second question lies in the question, "Where is God?" YAHWEH, being infinite Spirit is everywhere but in the unreceptive soul. Therefore, to be at one with Him is to be with Him or as Jesus said

*Heaven and Hell*

in Him. (John 17:21.) That is heaven.

At-one-ment requires total, persistent love. It is the absence of love that is hell. It is the choice to exclude the Father and so to isolate ourselves.

Heaven and hell are not places, they are states of being. Our choice is for now and forever after death of the body. We are living forever whether we want to or not. That is our nature and so not a choice. Our choice is solely in which state we shall live both now and forever after this earthly existence.

## IN SUMMARY

Would you free a child to all the privileges of an adult? Would you give such freedom to one who had never learned love or compassion for other persons or who had not learned the value of the rest of creation?

We are not the body. We are made in the image of our Father-Creator. We, too, are spirit with boundless minds.

After dealth of the body we have unlimited access to the minds of others and they to ours.

Is it any wonder that the Father confines us to the body until we have opportunity to learn what we must learn before we can be freeed into the presence of the Spirit Person and other "departed" spirit persons, that is, into Heaven?

# PART 7

## SON OF GOD, MESSIAH

# Chapter 24

## "Son of God" in the Bible

In the early mythologies it is said: "So it happened as mankind (haadham) began to multiply on the face of the earth (haadhamah) and daughters were born to them, the sons of God saw that the daughters of mankind were delightful and took to themselves wives from such as they chose." (Genesis 6:1f.)

The Psalms often contain remnants of ancient mythologies. E.g., in the 89th Psalm the poet is memorializing YAHWEH'S promise of perpetual security for the dynasty of David (verses 1-4 and 19-37.) It is an appeal for a restoration of the throne of David, calling upon YAHWEH to remember His promise.

Verses 38-51 are a word picture of the humiliating fall of Zedekiah to the Babylonians. The mythological remnant is used to proclaim the magnificence of YAHWEH'S superiority: "Let the heavens know thy transcendence, O YAHWEH...who among the clouds can be compared to YAHWEH? Who among the sons of God (aleem, may well be rendered "sons of the gods". Compare Psalm 29:1.) is like YAHWEH?...Thou didst crush Rehab like a carcass..." (89:5-10.)

This last sentence recalls the Babylonian epic of the defeat of Tiamat by Marduk. It appears to claim superiority of YAHWEH among the family of the gods. Job 1:6 and 2:1 are similar in the vision of a family of gods: "There was a day when the sons of God (of "the gods" eloheem) were coming to station themselves before YAHWEH..." This Zoroastrian passage goes on to say that "the adversary (hassatan) also was coming in their midst." At this point, it is not clear that this character is reckoned as one of the sons.

Job 38:7 poetically links the morning stars and the "sons of God." If this verse is taken to be synonymous parallelism, then the stars are being presented as sons. Psalm 82:6 reads: "I say, 'You are gods, sons of the Exalted One, all of you.'" Here, the poet is referring to the leaders of the people who serve as their judges. (Psalm 82:1-5.)

In Isaiah 43:6, YAHWEH says of His exiled people: "...bring my sons from afar and my daughters from the ends of the earth." He speaks similarly of Israel as His sons in Isaiah 45:11. So it is also in Ezekiel 21:10 (verse 15 in Hebrew) where YAHWEH warns of a sword of discipline coming upon Israel "my son" for their idolatry. Hosea used the same figure (11:1.)

It is normal for the people of Israel to be referred to in the singular as "Israel he." But Hosea 1:10 (Hebrew 2:1) uses the plural: "...it shall be said to them, 'sons of the living God.'" But he returns to the singular again in 13:13 in reference to Ephraim, a common representation for the Northern Kingdom.

It is not until II Samuel 7:14 that an individual is singled out for the title "son of YAHWEH". YAHWEH says: 'I am being to him for father and he is being to me for son..." The messianic psalms follow. E.g., Psalm 2:6f., "I have set (nasach) my king on Zion, my holy mountain...He (YAHWEH) said to me, 'my son you are, I this day have begotten you.'"

Although II Samuel refers to Solomon, from that time on in the Old Testament the reference is to one of the line of David anointed (messiahed) for the throne of Israel. He is always thought of as a mighty and vengeful conqueror of the nations and especially of Israel's oppressors as in Psalm 2:6-9.

In the story of the fiery furnace in Daniel, of the fourth person seen walking about in the flames with Shadrach, Meshach and Abednego, it is said: "...The appearance of the fourth is like [the] son of God." (Daniel 3:25 l'bar elaheen, Aramaic.)

The New Testament has an entirely different perception of the figure, "Son of God". Please note the following, chapter 25, in this regard. Jesus refused to be a king in the same sense of the Old Testament "son of God". When the people sought to make him king after he had fed them, he slipped away to hide himself: "Jesus knowing that they were about to come and carry him off to make him king, he withdrew again to the hills alone." (John 6:15.)

At his trial before the High Priest, he is asked if he is the "Christ, the son of the Blessed," i.e., YAHWEH. (Mark 14:61.) In Mark 14:62 he replies "I am." Luke 22:70 records the reply as, "You say that I am." Matthew 26:64 has only, "You say." In answer to Pilate's question, "Are you the king of the Jews?" Jesus replies evasively again as he did to the High Priest: "You say." (Mark 15:2 and Luke 23:3.) But according to Luke 23:4, this answer is to be taken as a denial. These reports leave us with some doubt as to what the response of Jesus was in any case. What we do know is that Jesus would not be the kind of messiah (son of God) the Old Testament and even the apocryphal writings portrayed him to be. Note the wrathful, vengeful figure presented in the book of Revelation.

The editor who gives us the present form of the gospel of John summarizes the entire purpose of that gospel as the means of persuading people to believe that "Jesus is the Christ, the son of God..." (John 20:31.) For the New Testament, "Christ" and "the son of God" are synonymous. In the Old Testament, the expression is similar only when preceded by the definite article. Otherwise, all the faithful are children of YAHWEH, each a "son of God."

# Chapter 25

# Messiah-Christos-Anointed

Here are three words all meaning the same thing. The first is Hebrew, the second Greek and the last from Old French which evolved from Latin. Literally, the root of the Hebrew verb (mashahc) means to smear or stroke with the hand, liquid or oil or paint. It is first used in the Bible in Genesis 31:13. Here YAHWEH is identifying Himself to Jacob as "the God of Bethel, where you anointed a pillar..."

The next occurrence is in Exodus 28:41 where Moses is instructed to anoint Aaron and his sons for the priesthood. In Leviticus the priests, who were to administer the religious colony that was to be established in Jerusalem, were guaranteed economic security by their anointing. (Leviticus 7:34-36.) Their anointing also gave them magical powers for atoning for the sins of the people, themselves and the ritual equipment. (Leviticus 16:32-34.)

Reference to anointing a king is first found where Jotham speaks of the people of Shechem making Abimelech their king in Judges 9:15. But the first king anointed in the Christian sense of Messiah, lord (or prince) and savior, is Saul (I Samuel 9:16.)

It is noteworthy that Jesus was never anointed in the same way as the kings from Saul and David onward. He was anointed by John the Baptist with water from the Jordan River as a sign of repentance. (Mark 1:4 and 9.) However, Like Saul (I Samuel 10:1-10) and David (I Samuel 16:13),

*Son of God, Messiah*

Jesus also is inspired by his anointing (Mark 1:9-12.)

It appears to be expected that, when one is YAHWEH'S true Messiah, He will have unusual powers. He will have an important role in the Creator's plans. The Christian view is similar to that of the Hebrew but parochial. It misses the fact that the writers in Babylon, who gave to us Second Isaiah, saw even Cyrus as a true Messiah of YAHWEH. (Isaiah 45:1ff.) By fixing a definite article before the word Messiah, as applied to Jesus, Christians fence off the word for dogmatic reasons.

The ethical prophets, Isaiah, Hosea, Amos and Micah, changed the Old Testament thought from their time onward. It was then possible for Jesus of Nazareth, a Jew, to have a marvelous effect upon all religions. In his brief ministry of three years, building on the ethical prophets, Jesus lived and taught so effectively that the world has never been the same since. This is so in spite of the fact that Jesus never presented anything new but one: he said: "A new commandment I give you, that you love one another even as I have loved you..." (John 13:34.)

Here is a man, a common man who grew up as an ordinary small town boy. As the eldest son, he was taught the trade of his father—a carpenter. When his mother was widowed, he was expected to look after his family consisting of four brothers and several sisters with his widowed mother. (Mark 6:2f.)

Like his father, Jesus was in a vocation that made him well known to his neighbors. It is understandable, therefore, that they did not accept him as a legitimate prophet let alone as the Messiah expected to rescue them from Roman oppression. (Luke 4:16-29.) The myths regarding his miraculous birth and spectacular miracles performed by him likely had their origin in an attempt to validate his messiahship among those who knew of his humble beginning.

It is not necessary to validate his ministry by such creations. The impact Jesus has had on the world is adequate proof of his right to the title "The Messiah." Of course, it can never fit the Old Testament expectations.

Even if there was truth to the rumor that the virgin birth was created to cover the gossip that Mary became pregnant by a Roman soldier, Jesus' ministry would be all the more validated. Even his lineage: incest of Jacob and his daughter-in-law, Ruth a Moabite wife of Boaz, adultery of

*Messiah-Christos-Anointed*

David with Bathseheba, and some of the most corrupt and ruthless kings in human history can have no place in judgment on the way he lived out his ministry.

All this would be to his credit in that he blossomed in spite of his lineage. As to the miracles attributed to him, one will find that these were made to duplicate those of Elijah and Elisha. How would he otherwise be made to appear greater than the greatest before him? If Caesar, Zoroaster and Buddha claim virgin birth, how else can he be made at least equal with those characters in that respect?

The virgin birth story reveals its legendary nature in the fact that the only Bible accounts (Luke 1:26ff. and Matthew 1:18ff.) are denied in those very same books by tracing Jesus' genealogy down from David through his father, Joseph. (Luke 3:23 and Matthew 1:16.) Paul, whose writings are the earliest in the New Testament, and Mark, the earliest of the gospels, knew nothing of it. By the time John's gospel got its present form, it was already forgotten. The myth of the virgin birth apparently was valued in the early Church only for the period of about 30 years between Mark's gospel (about 65 A.D.) and the Gospel of John (present form about 95 A. D.)

The manner of his birth is strictly immaterial. What is important is how he complied with the will of his God in his ministry through Gethsemane and the crucifixion. I sometimes think that people nurture these ideas of his uniqueness, beyond the single fact of his virtue, to excuse themselves from obedience to his "New Commandment". As I said in an earlier chapter, "Such people would complain, 'I can't be like him—he was born of a virgin!'"

As to the myths about what happened to the body of Jesus, the same can be said for the loss of track of the bodies of Moses and Elijah. Think what pagan shrines and relics their bodies would have become. Jesus' whole ministry was devoted to turning people's minds from idolatry of the physical to see more clearly the Spirit-Father-Creator.

As Jesus said to the Samaritan woman at the well—his first missionary—his first apostle—"...the hour is coming, in fact it's here now, when the true worshipper will worship the Father as spirit and truth, for such the Father seeks to worship Him." (John 4:23.)

There is hardly a human being of past or present who can honestly deny that the solution to all human problems is the Two Great Commandments (Deuteronomy 6:4f. and Leviticus 19:34.) applied as Jesus applied them. It is not until people begin to seek ways of avoiding Jesus' life as "the way" that the Church fails. As long as people walked and lived with Jesus, they never lost track of the Way.

But, when time is spent inventing dogmas and creeds about who and what he was, (i.e., exercises in religious philosophies called theology, christology, and ecclesiology) they begin to convince themselves that they are excused from living the Way. One has to have completely blinded himself to what is going on in the world honestly to believe that there is any excuse at all. As is plain to be seen, idolatry does horrible things to people's conscience and objectivity.

Jesus was not a messiah in the sense of the Old Testament ideas. Zechariah says: "...Lo, your king comes to you. Righteous and victorious is he, humble and riding on an ass..." (Zechariah 9:9.) Jesus was like that.

But the following verses (13 and 15) add: "I have bent Judah as my bow. I have made Ephraim its arrow. I will brandish your sons, O Zion, over your sons, O Greece, and wield you like a warrior's sword." "YAHWEH of hosts will protect them and they shall devour and tread down the slingers; and they shall drink their blood like wine and be full like a bowl..." Jesus was not at all like that.

Is it any wonder that Jews of his day could not accept him as Messiah? Their vision of Messiah was quite different from the role that Jesus chose to fulfill. Both Peter (Matthew 16:21-23) and Judas (Matthew 27:3f.), along with many others, made an honest mistake regarding the role of the messiah in the Father's plans.

# Chapter 26

# On the Second Coming ("Adventism")

This dogma arises out of a need to satisfy or support the position that messiah must be a great conquering hero. (Note the book of Revelation.) When one holds that Jesus was this messiah—since he would not be that kind of a superman in his first appearance—he must come again to fulfill that role.

The idea of reincarnation (a second stint on earth in the flesh) was not unheard of in Jesus' day. In reply to the question he offered to his disciples at Caesarea, Philippi, "Who do men say that I am?" (Mark 8:27) they replied, "John the Baptist; and others say Elijah; and others, one of the prophets." (Mark 8:28.) Among the last of the words of the book of Malachi (4:5) it is written: "Behold, I send to you Elijah the prophet before the great and awful day of YAHWEH comes."

Thus many people in Jesus' time looked for the coming of the Messiah to be preceded by a reincarnation of the prophet as a sign. It is to be expected, therefore, that some should ask Jesus, "Why do the scribes say that it is necessary for Elijah to come first?" (Mark 9:11.) Jesus replies: "Elijah does come first to restore all things." (Mark 9:12.) He goes on to say, "But I say to you that Elijah has come and they did to him whatever they wished..." (Mark 9:13.)

Matthew 17:13 adds the interpretation of these verses saying,

*Son of God, Messiah*

"Then the disciples understood that he (Jesus) spoke to them of John the Baptist." Similarly, King Herod, when he heard the report of Jesus' healing exploits, said: "John the Baptist, whom I beheaded has been raised." (Mark 6:16.)

But, in the gospels themselves, we are left with serious problems on this matter of Jesus' personal return. In discussing the cataclysmic events of the great day of judgment, Jesus speaks of the destruction of the temple, persecution of his followers and their flight from their homes. Then follows an apocryphal description of the universe in turmoil and the gathering of the scattered faithful. (Mark 13:3-27.)

In response to the question regarding when this is to take place, Jesus says: "Amen, I say to you that this generation shall not have passed away (A.V. translates "shall not pass", but this form is 2nd Aorist Subjunctive, not future) until all these things take place." (Mark 13:30.)

It is recorded in Matthew regarding the persecutions to be experienced by the disciples: "...I say to you, you shall not have fled through (in context of the first half of this verse; literally "completed" telesate) all the towns of Israel before the son of man shall have come." (2nd Aorist Subjunctive, Matthew 10:23.)

Mark 9:1 and Luke 9:27 and Matthew 16:28 all record Jesus as saying: "...Amen, I say to you, there are some of those standing here who shall not taste death until they shall have seen (again Aorist Subjunctive) the Kingdom of God having come in power."

With doubly emphasized negatives and Aorist Subjunctives used throughout these recorded sayings of Jesus, the writers certainly meant to underline the definiteness of these promises or proclamations made by Jesus. He and they expected the great day of YAHWEH, the once and forever establishment of the Kingdom of God, to take place during the lifetime of those to whom he was speaking. Since the "second coming" was a central sign of the arrival of the Kingdom, we must look to those historical events that indicate the fulfilment of Jesus' prophecies.

If one holds with those parts of the New Testament that see the Kingdom of God coming with the arrival of Jesus a second time, then he has problems with the numerous reported statements of Jesus that the Kingdom has already come. The Pharisees ask Jesus when the Kingdom is to come. He replies that it won't be with a lot of visible signs. He says

## On the Second Coming ("Adventism")

that this is so, "For behold the Kingdom of God is inside of you." (Luke 17:21.) The Greek word entos, here used, means exactly the opposite of ektos which means outside.

This saying makes good sense. A king to be a king must have subjects or he would be no more than a landholder. When people subject themselves to the will of YAHWEH, He becomes a king and not before. We are reminded here of YAHWEH'S words to Samuel (I Samuel 8:7): "...they have not rejected you, but they have rejected me that I should not be king over them." Only subjects make a king.

Upon sending out the seventy apostles to prepare the way for him, Jesus charges them to heal the sick and proclaim: "The Kingdom of God has come upon you." (Luke 10:9.) For those receiving the apostles, the word epi makes the statement even stronger than for those rejecting them. (Luke 10:11.) For those refusing the apostles, the Kingdom has only "come near." (angiken without the epi.)

When he is confronted by those who say that Jesus is casting out demons by the "lord of flies," he justifies his work as the work of God. Then he says: "But if it is by the finger of God that I cast out demons, then the Kingdom of God has enveloped you." (ephthasen Luke 11:20.)

In the collection of Jesus' sayings in Matthew, Jesus says: "Blessed are those having been persecuted for the sake of righteousness for theirs is the Kingdom of God." (Matthew 5:10.) All this makes the Kingdom immediate and certainly eliminates any need of a dogma of a "second coming" of Jesus in bodily form.

Looking to those historical events that led to a conclusion that Jesus always spoke figuratively when referring to his return, there is ample support in the Bible itself. One thing of great note took place within the lifetime of those to whom Jesus spoke. That was Pentecost in that upper room where the 120 were gathered. (Acts, chapter 2.)

The spirit that possessed Jesus literally possessed them all and transformed them, from a small band cringing in fear for their lives, into a powerful vocal group of evangelists. It was this small beginning that made it possible for Jesus' life to influence the entire world for good. Without them, Jesus would have been just another frustrated prophet. He would have been nobody's messiah.

The Church as the form of the kingdom of God was born that day at

*Son of God, Messiah*

Pentecost. Jesus was no longer on earth to bear the message of love and to do his work of healing humanity. Thus it was that Jesus came again—figuratively—in all those who were like him and who were and are properly called "Christians" (christianous Acts 11:26) or, by whatever name, choose to follow in his steps.

Jesus' figure of his second coming as likened to a flash of lightning that illuminated the entire sky (Luke 17:24) is very appropriate. Jesus was just one man. His disciples were many and they spread his truth over the whole earth. It is proper that the true (invisible) Church or Synagogue be spoken of as "The Body of Christ." He came again as he promised, in their time and in power. He is still here and still coming in all of his true followers and in those yet to be born anew.

As Paul said: "You, therefore, are the body of Christ and members individually." (I Corinthains 12:27.) In this entire chapter of I Corinthians, Paul is laboring to make clear how those taken over by the Spirit become the Christ to do all that Jesus came to do.

They are not alone, but as a part of the whole along with each and every other true "Christian". (Incidentally, since the word "Christian" is an adjective meaning "Christ-like," it seems we would all do well to consider this fact before making any use of the word or of applying it to ourselves.)

# Chapter 27

# King of Kings and Lord of Lords and Subjects

When the priests of Josiah wrote, "For YAHWEH your God is God of gods and Lord of lords..." (Deuteronomy 10:17) it is impossible that they could have expected this title to be applied one day to a human—even one of His sons in the Old Testament sense of Messiah. Usually one can find plenty of contradictions in the Old Testament itself. But this is not one of them. For such a title is reserved exclusively for the Father-Creator in the first three-fourths of the Christian Bible.

That YAHWEH was always to be the only king of the Hebrews is strongly affirmed in the events leading to the sinful choice of a human king in the days of Saul. "Then YAHWEH said to Samuel, 'Give heed to the voice of the people, to all they are saying to you, for they have not rejected you (as their prophet) but they have rejected me from being king over them.'" (I Samuel 8:7.)

All the rest of the history of the Old Testament period, the devastating results of interposing a human between them and their God, proved how completely wrong it is. This is equally true whether it be of a king or a priest or any other intermediary. Things may go well while the go-between is a benevolent individual, but humans do not occupy such an office forever. Sooner or later another Jezebel and Ahab or Athaliah

*Son of God, Messiah*

or a Manasseh comes along and all hell breaks loose upon the society.

That the Father-Creator is always to be the only king is affirmed and reaffirmed again and again throughout the Old Testament. Even as the book of Deuteronomy is properly rendered: "For YAHWEH is your Strength, the Power of the mighty ones and Lord of lords, the powerful, the great, the mighty and the wonderful One who does not show partiality and who does not take a bribe." (Deuteronomy 10:17.) So the psalmists join in with such words as: "YAHWEH is King forever and ever..." (Psalm 10:16) and "Who is this King of glory? YAHWEH strong, even mighty..." "Who is this King of glory? YAHWEH of Hosts..." (Psalm 24:8 and 10.) See one more among many others: "...for YAHWEH remains (wayashebh) King forever." (Psalm 29:10.)

The prophet Isaiah echoes the words of the psalmists (or vice versa.) In the event of Isaiah's call, he cries out in fear for his life: "...the King, YAHWEH of Hosts, my eyes have seen." (Isaiah 6:5.) His followers in Babylon say that YAHWEH Himself proclaims: "I am YAHWEH your holy One, Creator of Israel, your king." (Isaiah 43:15.)

Even the apocryphal book of Daniel, late as it is in Hebrew history, speaks similarly putting in the mouth of King Nebuchadnezzar the words: "Of a truth your God is the Power of the mighty ones and Lord of Kings..." (Daniel 2:47.) Then Darius is made to say: "I set forth a decree that in all the dominion of my reign that there be (lehewon, Aramaic) fear and trembling before the God of Daniel, for He is the living God and enduring perpetually...and His dominion is forever" (or "to the end" gadh-sopha, Aramaic. Daniel 6:26, Aramaic 6:27.)

The writer of the first epistle to Timothy carries on the Old Testament tradition. Speaking of Jesus' appearing that will be made possible by YAHWEH, he says of YAHWEH: "...by the blessed and only Ruler, the King of kings and Lord of lords, who alone has immortality, dwelling in unapproachable light, whom no man has seen—no one is able to see..." (I Timothy 6:15f.)

It is not until some 35 to 40 years later that the title is visited upon Jesus and that is by the vengeful writer of the so-called Apocalypse of John or Revelation. (Revelation 19:16.) This has been popularized by classical music under the title "The Messiah". The music is beautiful and inspiring but it is hardly fair use of the Bible.

The book of Revelation is not a good place to look for the pure and gentle thoughts of the man who made primary the love and commitment to the will of the loving Father that took him to and beyond the Cross.

However, for one—even YAHWEH—to be a king, he must have willing subjects. Otherwise He is only a land holder and manipulator of puppets. This is why I dislike the ritual testimony of those who wear the clerical collar which is no more nor less than a symbol of slavery. For anyone to love, he must be free. Love cannot be compelled or it is not love.

Understanding and accepting Exodus 34:6 makes possible acceptance and commitment to the Two Great Commandments. Those who willingly submit to the will of the Father-Creator here set forth are His subjects. It is only by this means that He can be King.

This is why Jesus, being asked by the Pharisees when the Kingdom of God would come, replied: "The Kingdom of God is not coming with observation. Nor will they say, 'Lo! Here it is,' or 'There!' for the Kingdom of God is inside of you." (Luke 17:20f.)

# PART 8

# ON THE PHYSICAL RESURRECTION

# Chapter 28

# Some Questions Raised By the Dogma of the Physical Resurrection

"Enoch walked with God and he was not, for God took (laqahc) him. (Genesis 5:24.) "...and Elijah (aliyahu in Hebrew) was going (or "was caused to go") up the heavens by a storm wind." (II Kings 2:11.) "The medium of Endor said to Saul: 'An old man is coming up...' and Saul knew it was Samuel..." (I Samuel 28:14) "Then Samuel said to Saul, 'Why have you disturbed me by bringing me up?'" (I Samuel 28:15.) Jesus took Peter, James and John up a high mountain and "there appeared to them Elijah with Moses; and they were talking to Jesus." (Mark 9:2-4.)

How can Jesus be the first to be resurrected as the creeds insist? In his discussion with the Sadducees, who did not believe in the resurrection of the dead, Jesus said, "For when they rise from the dead, they neither marry nor are given in marriage, but are like the messengers (angeloi) in the heavens." and "...have you not read in the Book of Moses about the bush, how God spoke to him saying, 'I am the God of Abraham and the God of Isaac and the God of Jacob'? He is not a God of the dead but of the living." (Mark 12:25-27.)

Paul testifies: "...Christ died on account of sins, according to the scriptures, and that he was buried, and he was raised (or awakened, egagertai from egeiro) on the third day according to the scriptures and that he appeared to over 500 brethren all at once, out of whom most now remain, although some have fallen asleep. Then he appeared to James and all the apostles." (I Corinthians 15:3-7.)

The appearance of Jesus to Paul apparently was a vision. Many see Acts 9:3-9 as a vivid account of a grand mal epileptic seizure that accompanied or produced the vision of Jesus' appearance to Paul.

Since the bodies of Jesus and the malefactor crucified with him were there before the eyes of all the people when these two died, how can it be taught that the body is involved in their presence in "paradise" that very day?

Are not the accounts of Jesus' appearances more like those of Moses and Elijah in the transfiguration recorded in Mark 9:2-4? Here the dead appear and disappear in a cloud.

The two on the road to Emmaus walked in Jesus' presence but did not recognize him all that time as they conversed with him on the way. When they did recognize him as he broke bread, Jesus mysteriously disappeared. (Luke 24:13-31.)

When these two disciples were telling their experience to the eleven, Jesus suddenly appeared among them. Luke writes: "But they were startled and frightened and they supposed they were seeing a spirit." (Luke 24:37.)

Traditions grow and grow and change in the process of oral transmission. In their enthusiasm to convince skeptics, no doubt additions were made to the message of the disciples that Jesus lives as do all who have passed from this life by death of the body.

The earliest writings about these things are the letters of Paul. His experience of Jesus surviving death of the body was his vision on the road to Damascus. So he wrote to the Corinthians trying to sort out and separate the earthly body from that of the existence of persons following release from the body. (I Corinthians 15:44.) He climaxes his effort with the statement: "I tell you this, brethren, flesh and blood are not able to inherit the Kingdom of God, nor does the perishable substance (phthora) inherit the imperishable (aphtharsian). (I Corinthians 15:50.)

Whatever the truth behind the events regarding the body of Jesus

## Questions Raised By the Dogma of the Physical Resurrection

after the crucifixion, it is totally immaterial as to the effects his short ministry had on the world. In the later gospel of Matthew (written some fifty years after the event) it was suggested that Jesus' followers might steal the body in an attempt to deceive the people into believing that his body was actually resurrected. (Matthew 27:62-64.)

Although Matthew adds an earthquake (Matthew 28:2) to roll back the stone, sealing the tomb, to the story as told by Mark, both he and Luke apparently used the written gospel of Mark as a foundation of their accounts. It is plain to be seen that both quote Mark exactly in some of the same passages.

The writer of the Gospel of John adds a nebulous account of Mary Magdalene conversing with one she thinks to be the gardener, but who turns out to be Jesus. All these accounts of Jesus' appearances have aspects pointing to visions.

Only the Gospel of John contains the account of Jesus' sudden appearance among the disciples gathered behind locked doors and windows. Jesus appears to have materialized in their midst or to have passed through the walls of the building. (John 20:19f.) This gospel got its present form some seventy years after the event. It raises a number of questions regarding what the story tellers actually saw.

"Just as day was breaking, Jesus stood on the shore  Yet the disciples did not know it was Jesus." The account goes on recounting how Jesus tells the fishermen to try again. The result is a miraculous catch of fish. (John 21:4ff.) Then they are invited to share breakfast with him.

Finally, in John 21:12, "Now none of the disciples dared ask him, 'Who are you?' They knew it was the lord." There was always this doubt, this wondering about what was seen. (Incidentally, Luke places this event of the miraculous catch of fish at the beginning of Jesus' ministry. (Luke 5:4ff.)

The fact that the Church, down through the ages, has joined in these attempts to validate (one way or another) the physical resurrection and the appearances of Jesus has been keeping it so occupied with wasteful and fruitless labors. So that it has not devoted itself to the proper effort to lead disciples to do the work Jesus called his followers to do.

It is easy to avoid loving each other as Jesus loved. It is not easy to live in this modern age of technology in gratitude to the Father-Creator.

## On The Physical Resurrection

If one has money and a finger to punch buttons on a telephone—"Who needs God?"

Loving YAHWEH is a chore and distracts from the pursuit of more wealth and physical convenience and comfort and social rank or approval.

So mankind seeks to avoid a sense of guilt by making religion too confusing and therefore too difficult. Jesus, whom we are to follow precisely, is made special and remote, thus providing excuses for failure to live as he lived. The dogma of the physical resurrection is one of these devious subterfuges.

Probably the most devastating question raised by this dogma is that one used by the Sadducees against the Pharisees in Mark 12:18ff. (See also Luke 20:27ff. and Matthew 22:23ff.) The woman had seven husbands. "In the resurrection, which of them is she to be wife?..." (Mark 12:23.) The Pharisees always lost the argument about whether there is any life after death of the body at this point. Jesus had to set them both straight by saying, in effect, that life after this one on earth is not physical.

Those who have crossed the threshold of clinical death already know that this is true from their own experience of looking upon their bodies apart after leaving them.

What often concerns the bereaved is that there be an assurance that we shall know and be known by each other. Any other than a self and other consciousness in the afterlife would make no sense whatsoever. The poet who gave us the book of Job would be a false prophet. For then there would be no justice, since it is plain to be seen that justice is not always fulfilled in this earthly existence. The proper song would be: "Eat drink and be merry now for tomorrow we shall be annihilated." "Get all the gusto you can and let all others take care of themselves." There is far too much of this practiced in our age as it is.

The most pitiful person is one bereaved of a loved spouse and who believes the spouse is looking over his or her shoulder in any new marriage relationship that might be established. I often think that those who have gone before get lots of chuckles over the misguided ideas that are rooted in belief in a physical resurrection. You and I should be quite concerned over the unnecessary suffering the bereaved undergo from such irrational and destructive ideas.

One other attitude that is generated by such false Christian teachings

## Questions Raised By the Dogma of the Physical Resurrection

and that seems totally absent in the Old Testament is the fear of death. The folk there appear to face death quite matter-of-factly. Their writers do not mention fear of death—only regret when it comes too soon. Jacob rejoices at having been able to see his grandchildren and to parcel out his accumulated power and wealth to his children. "Then Jacob, having finished charging his sons, and having gathered his feet to the bed and expiring, thus was gathered to his people." (Genesis 49:33.)

Aaron (Numbers 33:38) and Moses (Numbers 27:12f. and Deuteronomy 34:5) similarly face their demise as the natural order of things. Of course there would be no concern about death when there is total annihilation of the individual as a result. My experience, in sitting with many near death, is that fear comes only to those who believe that death of the body is not all there is.

The creedal position that Jesus saves from dread of physical death only applies to those who know they are right (atoned) with the will of the Father-Creator. Those who expect a physical life after death will have many concerns related to physical aging and pain along with a great potential for boredom.

If you can accept it as truly the word of Jesus, in the Gospel of John the answer is clear. Jesus said: "If a person loves me he will keep my word and my Father will love him and I will come to him and make my dwelling with him." (John 14:23.) If Jesus was physically resurrected, how can he dwell with each and all the faithful?

# Chapter 29

# On the Book of Job
# (The Old Testament)

If all the books of the Old Testament were to be taken away from me but one, I would choose to keep the book of Job. Although It was clearly composed for one purpose, it contains the entire spiritual message of the Old Testament and most of the New Testament. Perhaps it lacks the vision of Exodus 34:6 and the Two Great Commandments, but it provides fully all the rest of Bible truth.

I use the word "composed" purposely, for the book is wonderfully constructed poetry. Although it sings of the infinite character of YAHWEH and the beauty and marvelous nature of His creation, the mechanical perfection of the structure of the book has never been surpassed in human creations.

In spite of its orderly perfection, the content of the book is priceless and without a peer in its powerful presentation of the wonderful magnificence of YAHWEH. In chapters 38-41, the poet calls attention to all that is marvelous about creatures and the world in which they live. His words are vivid pictures of the breath-taking splendor of the character-revealing work of the Creator who nevertheless has intimate concern for all He has created.

The author is heavily oppressed by the misconception of the Old Testament society that all those at one with YAHWEH have good health, wealth, and long life. He has Job protest: "Have you not asked those traveling the way, and do you not regard their assurance that, for the day of calamity, the wicked one is spared, that for the day of the passover he is borne along? Who declares to his face his way? So who compensates him for what he has done?" (Job 21:29-31.)

Job's three friends are no help. In fact the poet gives Job the upper hand in all three rounds of debate. What truths these three characters opposing Job do present are swallowed up in their mechanical condemnation of Job: Job is ill, suffering and poverty stricken. Therefore he must have been doing something terribly wrong.

These three "friends", who represent the society, fail to help Job with specifics so that he might know what he has done wrong. They antagonize the poet mightily so that he explodes with the words that he gives to the young man, Elihu, the true hero of the poem.

In so doing, the poet incidentally adds another accomplishment in that he denies the Old Testament tradition that age and wisdom are necessarily paired. "Certainly it is the spirit in mankind, the breath of the Almighty that causes them to understand. It is not the many that are wise, nor the old that discern justly." (Job 32:8f.) Thus he pronounces the fallibility of the two sources of the "last word."

The three friends of Job are assigned names that suit the poet's opinion of the wrong position taken by the Hebrew society. Eliphaz means "my god is find gold". Zophar means "chirp or peep". Bildad means "Bel has loved", a pagan name.

Job's name is also appropriate to the character in the poem. It means "object of enmity" or, if Aramaic, "he who turns".

The hero of the poem, Elihu, is named appropriately "my God is He." So in the names of his characters, the poet sets the scene for his message. The three friends represent the false position of the Hebrew society or "the many."

Job embodies the role of the good people who suffer. Elihu is the voice of the poet in protest. He alone names specifically the areas where Job needs correction in spite of his otherwise virtuous life. (Job 32:1, conceit; 34:9, blasphemy; 34:31f., stubbornness; 34:37, rebellion.) That this is the help that Job needed is seen in his sincere repentance in 42:1-6.

# On the Book of Job (The Old Testament)

Note how quickly "Satan" is disposed of here as elsewhere in the Old Testament. Some Zoroastrian individual added the prose portions in the first two chapters. The incompatibility of these two chapters with the poem itself is quite evident. The old devil disappears from Job 2:10 onward.

Sin is between the sinner and YAHWEH. There is no place for intermediaries or an outside personal force of evil. (See further part 5, chapter 20, Satan, That Old Devil, The Serpent.)

The prose portion of chapter 42 of Job is likewise an attempt by some editor to discredit the poet's work. The portion that follows 42:10 is quite obviously meant to undo all that the poet has achieved in his poem. He has successfully presented his case, proving that justice is not completed in this life. His opponents take their final lick by making editorial additions to the poem.

The observable facts are on the side of the poet. So they can never detract from the remarkable message and literary perfection of the labors of this talented poet. The poetry begins and ends the true part of the poem. The prose portions are no more than a clumsy attempt to corrupt the poet's message.

# Chapter 30

# Who Wrote the Gospel of John? (The New Testament on the Resurrection and Love)

I would say that Lazarus did. The gospel itself shows us that he alone could be the "disciple whom Jesus loved."

But this gospel has been supplemented and grossly corrupted by an editor of a greatly different viewpoint. The editor could hardly have known anything of Jesus first hand. He was not steeped in Hebrew as Lazarus would have been. He sounds very much like the writers of the Alexandrian community who gave us the Septuagint and many allegorical writings.

Writers like Plycrates, Irenaeus and Origen of the second and third centuries A.D. proposed John, the son of Zebedee, as the author of this gospel. Following them, most people have blissfully accepted him as the "disciple whom Jesus loved" and as the author of the book.

There were a few dissenters along the way, however. Eusibius of Caesarea (260-340 A. D.) proposed "the Elder" of II and III John, whom he took to be a disciple or a scribe of John, the son of Zebedee. Many have made way for this idea by saying that John the apostle was behind the writing as one who dictated the material.

Some have proposed that the author is a John of Ephesus who had been exiled to Patmos. They thus make the author of the gospel and the three letters the same as the writer of Revelation. However, radical differences between Revelation and the rest preclude any possibility of all having the same author.

Revelation is written by someone who tries to express himself in Greek while thinking in Hebrew or Aramaic—very likely a Christian Pharisee. Grammatical syntax and idiom of the gospel and the three letters are (in their present form) Greek thought in Greek, a characteristic of the editor of the gospel.

Those scholars who carefully examine all the historical evidence must admit that outside material, i.e., anything outside the gospel itself, leaves us with no possibility of a sound conclusion as to authorship. The best that can be said from all this material is that he was an unknown evangelist.

Looking within the book, one must accept the author's signature in John 21:20 and 24. It is the "disciple whom Jesus loved", whomever that may be. To find the author of this gospel, one does not need any more information than that found in the book itself. The evidence is incontrovertible.

There is hardly a chance that the son of Zebedee could be the beloved disciple. It is true that John was one of the three favored among the twelve. (However little is recorded of any of the twelve except Peter after the death of Jesus. We have none of them as direct producers of New Testament writings.)

On special occasions Jesus takes the three, Peter, James and John apart with him: (1) when he goes to heal the daughter of the ruler of a synagogue (Mark 5:37); (2) in the transfiguration (Mark 9:2); (3) in Gethsemane just before he is betrayed and arrested (Mark 14:32f.) But there is nothing in the Fourth Gospel to set John apart from the other two. All three are fishermen, rough and impetuous.

James and John are rebuked for suggesting they call fire down from heaven to destroy an entire village in Samaria for not receiving Jesus (Luke 9:51-56.) This kind of attitude earned them the name "sons of thunder" (Mark 3:17.) It hardly attests to a loving or lovable nature.

John demonstrates a lack of understanding of Jesus' love that transcends jealousy when he stops a man from casting our demons in

Jesus' name (Mark 9:38-40.) Then it is he and his brother James who seek positions of favor and dominance over the others of the twelve (Mark 10:35-40.) This certainly did not endear them to the rest of the twelve. (Mark 10:41.)

There is only one who can possibly fit the title, "the disciple whom Jesus loved". That is Lazarus, the brother of Martha and Mary. It is inevitable that Jesus would be close to and especially loved by this family. Jesus had saved Mary from a life in the streets. As he said of her: "...her sins, which are many, are forgiven, for she loved much; but he who is forgiven little, loves little." (Luke 7:47.)

The author of the Fourth Gospel says: "It was Mary who anointed the Lord with ointment and wiped his feet with her hair whose brother Lazarus was ill." (John 11:2.)

This gospel makes certain that the special love Jesus had for Lazarus is known. He records this three times in chapter 11 alone. Verse 3, "So the sisters sent to him saying, 'Lord, he whom you love is ill.'" Verse 5, "Now Jesus loved Martha and her sister and Lazarus." Verses 35f., "Jesus wept. So the Jews said, 'See how he loved him!'"

It was not customary for leaders of the people to associate with common folk, especially with a family that had a member of Mary's reputation. But here we find them coming to mourn the death of Lazarus. Obviously, he was an important person in the city of Jerusalem. (John 11:18f.)

Another example of his importance is seen in that when Jesus is taken before the high priest, Peter had to remain outside while, of "another disciple," it is said: "...as this disciple was known to the high priest, he entered the court of the high priest along with Jesus." (John 18:15.) He was no ordinary, uneducated person as Jesus and the twelve were considered to be.

There is a passage that casts a shadow on our inference from the above passage. On another occasion, when Jesus and his disciples went up to Jerusalem to observe the Passover, the leaders of the people were disturbed by the fact that many people had gathered to see not only Jesus but also Lazarus. And it is said: "So the chief priests planned to put Lazarus also to death." (John 12:10.)

Even if this was not the work of the editor, the very fact that Jesus had been seized and was about to be condemned would have taken the pressure off of Lazarus so that he would have been welcomed into the high priest's house.

I think that all of chapter 12, as is the case of some others, is mainly the work of the editor because of its inconsistencies and the loveless vindictiveness it shows toward Judas in verses 4 through 7. It is this kind of gross conflict in attitude that separates the author and the editor in this gospel.

That Jesus had a special relationship with Lazarus's family is seen in that, when visiting Jerusalem, it was his custom to stay with Lazarus and his sisters at their home in Bethany which was near Jerusalem. It is his more intimate acquaintance with Jesus that leads the beloved disciple to emphasize the passages on agape love, that totally selfless devotion that was so unique that it needed a separate, special word. It parallels in many respects the special word ahabh in the Old Testament used frequently of YAHWEH'S love. The fact that the Fourth Gospel uses agape many more times than all the other gospels combined indicates a special comprehension of Jesus and his love.

It is significant that Lazarus' gospel is the only one to report Jesus' "new commandment". (John 13:34.) He alone records Jesus' words, "This is my commandment, that you love one another as I have loved you. Greater love has no man than this, that he lay down his life for his friends." (John 15:12f.)

Only he records the dialogue Jesus had with Peter in which it is revealed that Peter just could not grasp the depth of the reality of agape. Peter appears to be limited in his understanding to the family love embodied in philia. (John 21:15ff.) Only Lazarus could grasp the full meaning of this dialogue and so made it an important part of his gospel.

Only Lazarus could catch the full meaning of Jesus' words "that you love one another as I have loved you," and so made it, too, a part of his gospel. Lazarus would be the one, if any, to know the truth of the statement, "Fear does not exist in agape. But perfect (or mature) agape casts our fear..." (I John 4:18.)

Christianity could not exist without the depth of the experience and understanding of this dear friend of Jesus. The true meaning of Jesus' life would have been missed without the gospel of the "disciple whom Jesus loved," even imbedded as it is in a violently edited work.

But one so close to the master teacher and who was a well respected Jew would surely not portray Jesus as a man who taught in mysteries and was so confusing that his disciples could not understand him. Jesus' parables would not be to confound, but to make his message clear.

It is my conviction that the gospel of Lazarus was the clearest, plainest and simplest of all the gospels. It was probably the earliest and so the only one to include the time of the three years of Jesus' ministry instead of a few months of it as the other gospels do. What is left of it still reveals a uniqueness in that it plumbs the depth of understanding of love applied as Jesus lived it.

Why then the garbled account of the first chapter of the Fourth Gospel? The personification of the word (logos) is an abstraction made into a person, a technique that comes from the Greeks. Philo of Alexandria was a leader in an attempt to allegorize the Old Testament to adapt it to the gentile culture.

The thriving community in Alexandria had lost much of its Hebrew qualities, so much so that the Old Testament had to be translated into the common Greek language for them. And this could not be an accurate translation, but, like most modern translations into English, a paraphrase. Its ideas are made to fit the minds of people who do not appreciate the truths in the original Hebrew. Religion for such people has its value in esoteric mysteries rather than in truths to live by. It is an escape from moral responsibility.

A good example of this style is found in the relatively late portion of Proverbs. Here the writer does with wisdom (hcachmah, Proverbs 8:23-9:11) much the same as the editor has done with logos in John. Another example of garbling is the discussion of communion or the "Lord's Supper" in John 6:48-63, in which the disciples are not only confused but offended.

The Jesus Lazarus knew (and the one I know) did not go about confusing and offending those who loved him and sought honestly to understand his way and follow it. In that very passage, only one verse can be from the master teacher—verse 63: "It is the spirit that gives life, the flesh is absolutely no help. The words that I speak to you are spirit and life."

## On The Physical Resurrection

The environment of this passage also is teaching a completely un-Christian form of fatalism. (Note especially 6:44.) In fact, the passage from Jeremiah 31:31-34 referred to in John 6:45 demands plain teaching, for that is YAHWEH'S promise given there. Not only does the editor garble the good news in the Fourth Gospel, but you will find many contradictions. These are surely the result of the evidence that we have here of two writers of opposite points of view.

It is tragic that we do not have Lazarus' gospel as it was before it fell into the hands of the editor. Had it not been for Lazarus' sensitivity to the quality and power of Jesus' love as he lived it, it could hardly have shown through in the gospel in spite of that violence done by the editor.

Also, without the one who understood agape so well, we would still be seeking answers to the question, "What must I do to inherit eternal life?" (Mark 10:17.) Multitudes died on Roman crosses, but only one loved the way Jesus loved.

Appropriately, the climax of the evidence that Lazarus is the "disciple whom Jesus loved" is found in the closing scenes of the gospel. Peter and this disciple ran to the tomb upon notification that Jesus was not there. The beloved disciple, being younger, outran Peter and arrived first. But he already knew what to expect as he had once left a tomb himself. He did not rush right in as Peter did when he arrived. (John 20:2-8.)

Note that this disciple whom Jesus loved is never identified as an apostle or as one of the twelve. He was a unique one among Jesus' disciples.

Finally, of whom would there be curiosity about how long he would live except the one Jesus revived and brought forth from the tomb? Of what person other than Lazarus would there possibly have been a rumor that he was not to die? (John 21:23.) As the author tells us: "This is the disciple who is bearing witness to these things, and who has written these things..." (John 21:24.) His name is Lazarus, the brother of Martha and Mary.

# PART 9

## MATURE RELIGION

# Chapter 31

# The Golden Thread

What we are talking about here is the history of YAHWEH'S creative activity and human response and religious development under revelation. We are not so naive or unacquainted with human behavior as to believe that the Creator's success with mankind has been a straight line of progression from ignorance and superstition to religious perfection. No doubt that is the way YAHWEH, in His infinite wisdom and goodness, would like it.

The Golden Thread is an overall perspective of what has been revealed to humans and grasped at one time or another so as to permit that growth from ignorance to a full and true knowledge of YAHWEH and His will.

The Golden Thread is like an imaginary line that stretches from the depths of human ignorance of religion and (on its upper end) disappears in the infinite perfection of YAHWEH'S very being. It portrays gems of understanding caught by religious seekers from the beginning to the present.

It also anticipates achievements of the future. But the freedom the Creator has given to the human creature precludes a careful acquisition and acceptance of all that has been revealed. Even some of the most diligent and devoted seekers among the Jewish leaders of Jesus' day missed some of the most meaningful parts of this revelation. (E.g., John 3:1-12.)

## Mature Religion

The Bible is a running account of human religious development. But there are many ups and downs, advances and regressions. Not all humans have availed themselves of the knowledge and insights set before them by the Creator's many approaches to self-revelation. We know from experience how often a child considers adult wisdom to be foolishness. Sometimes, after a child passes through his teens, he wonders how his parents became so wise after appearing so foolish before. At other times, a well-taught child goes to his spiritual, physical or moral destruction because he never did catch on to the value of advice from experience.

We often see this happening in Bible accounts of the successes and failures of the various prophets and spiritual leaders. It is easy for a reader of the Bible to get the idea that the whole society (or a major portion of it) went along with these heroes of the Book. It is just as easy to mistakenly view the Bible as an accurate account of the life of all the people.

But this is what one might call prejudice or careless reading. One has to ignore a lot of the prophets' words to believe that they were carefully heeded. Listen to Jeremiah: "Woe is me, my mother, that you bore me, a man of strife and a man of contention to all the earth. I have not lent and they have not lent to me, [yet] they all curse me." (Jeremiah 15:10.)

Isaiah reports the words of YAHWEH: "...Sons I have increased and raised up, but they have rebelled against me." (Isaiah 1:2.)

Amos overflows with bitter frustration for the waywardness of the people. He says that their hope in the day of YAHWEH is misplaced for their wickedness is so extreme that that day will be for their destruction, not for the punishment of their enemies. (Amos 5:18ff.)

It is like the making of laws. If no one ever did what was legislated against, the law would not have been necessary in the first place. So we have frequent condemnations of Israel pronounced by their religious leaders. These condemnations would not have been made necessary if all or most of the people were doing well in the sight of YAHWEH.

Still, in spite of all this, there is the Golden Thread of a consistently progressing grasp of truths that run through the Bible as a whole. It begins long after the crude beginnings of primitive animism. There it was thought that spirits inhabit all inanimate objects. Accidents encountered with such objects were taken to be an attempt of the spirits to communicate with humans. It was up to those involved to figure out what to do to please the spirit.

Here we see the dawn of a belief that a power greater than man wished to communicate with him. As ingenious individuals were recognized as having better than average success with such incidents, witch doctors were born. This stifled YAHWEH'S efforts at self-revelation for a time.

From there the Bible takes up the story of the religious development of humans such as it has been. Early on, gods were made in the image of man. The mythologies and most of the peoples contacted by the Hebrews had their own man-like gods. In fact, we find remnants of such religious ideas in Genesis 6:1-4 and occasional poetic references in the Psalms.

Generally, it was only such individuals as were designated priests (evolved from the primitive witch doctor) who knew how to, or were permitted to communicate with the gods.

Abraham's family, representing the nomadic YAHWEH worshippers, brings us a new view of a Creator who is transcendent person and who communicates directly with any listening human.

Then there is a long period of regression where only the designated individuals dared approach this infinite being. He accumulated many human characteristics again. Much of the Bible portrays Him as wrathful, vengeful, jealous and making mistakes that must be corrected by wise men such as Moses. (E.g., Numbers 14:11-20.)

Still, with all this, we see glimpses of truth accumulating along the way. In Abraham's religion, we see an all-powerful but careful Person who communicates directly with receptive humans. With Jacob, we learn that YAHWEH is not limited to the Promised Land. Under Moses at Sinai, we find a covenantal relationship that requires strong discipline and meticulous loyalty to the one and only infinite God.

A special people wandered a long time in the wilderness being molded and remolded to become a means by which YAHWEH might reveal to all humanity what the true and only God is really like. This people was to become the means by which His will was made clear both negatively and positively.

In their subsequent history, as a people of peculiar spiritual insights,

## Mature Religion

they had deep and lasting effects on all other peoples. So they were established on the main highway crossroads of the sea and caravan routes of the civilized world of that day. Thus their peculiar religious understanding could be passed on to the whole world.

It was not without great cost to these servants (willing or otherwise) of YAHWEH. As the scribes in Babylon recorded it in Isaiah 43:10, YAHWEH says that the nations all witness to their gods, but "'You are my witnesses,' says YAHWEH, 'even my servant whom I have chosen...'" They had, for many generations, tenaciously clung to their belief in the Creator-Father at the crossroads of the world in spite of the fact that one great power after another rolled across them like a monster steam-roller.

Egypt came up from the south. Assyria came down from the north—Egypt up from the south and Babylon down form the north—then the Greeks and finally the Romans. Each in turn tried unsuccessfully to stamp out the Hebrew religion as the only means of stabilizing their hold on the land.

It was this pressure by the pagans that united and strengthened YAHWEH'S attraction for the minds of His people. Poets' and prophets' deep revelations of YAHWEH'S character and personhood were caught and recorded by scribes down through the ages, a period of violent molding. Each added another precious bead to the Golden Thread.

In spite of the terrible violence through which the Hebrews developed, more marvelous insights were added as beads on the Golden Thread. "...YAHWEH is YAHWEH, a Mighty One, compassionate and gracious, patient and the very substance of steadfast love (hcesedh) and truth." (Exodus 34:6.)

This is especially remarkable in the light of His infinite power. "When I see your heavens and the work of your fingers, the moon and the stars which you have made, what is humankind (enosh) that you keep him in your thoughts—even the son of man (ben-adham) that you look after him. Yet, you make him lacking little from [thyself] (eloheem)..." (Psalm 8:3-5.)

The scribes in Babylon recorded YAHWEH'S words: "I—I—am YAHWEH and besides me there is no savior." (Isaiah 43:11.)

It is to the great pagan emperor of Babylon that it was given to

*The Golden Thread*

proclaim YAHWEH'S infinite power: "All the dwellers of the earth are considered nothing. He does as He chooses among the host of heaven and among all the dwellers of the earth. So none can smite His hand or say to Him, 'What have you done?'" (Peal Perfect, Aramaic; Daniel 4:35.)

Out of their experience, the Creator with all His infinite power, is seen as a loving Father to His people. (Hosea 1-3 and 11.) By the time of the reforms under King Josiah, the Hebrew creed was formed: "Listen Israel! YAHWEH is our Strength. YAHWEH is one. And you shall love YAHWEH your God (or Power, eloheem) with all your mind, with all your soul, and with all your strength (or most or being, m'odh, Deuteronomy 6:4f.)" This commandment was given to govern all thoughts in their entire waking moments. It was to be taught perpetually parent to child in every generation. (Deuteronomy 6:6-9.)

It is remarkable that throughout the Hebrew history, the tragic results of people insisting on a mediator between them and their God and between them and their enemies, appears to have been ignored. Priests and kings were kept in spite of their terrible, destructive effects on religious development, both personal and social or national.

The people's fear of YAHWEH had to be dispelled before they could dispense with priests. They had to take full responsibility personally for the welfare of their society before they could undo their sin of insisting on a king and denying YAHWEH'S will for a theocracy. (I Samuel 8:7; 12:12, 19.)

It was not until Jesus of Nazareth that the full possibility of obeying the first of the Two Great Commandments was achieved, or that Exodus 34:6 could be fully understood. In order to be able to love Him, YAHWEH had to be seen as lovable. Only when Exodus 34:6 becomes an experience of an individual is that possible.

Hosea portrays vividly the experience of a kindly, sensitive man learning the depths of YAHWEH'S love through suffering that he endured in loving a wayward wife so much that he could not let her go. This is the way he learned how YAHWEH feels about His wayward people.

Ezekiel, well acquainted with the suffering of an exile, records YAHWEH'S compassionate cry: "'Cast away from you all the rebellions you have committed against me and make for yourselves a new mind and a new spirit, for why are you dying, O House of Israel? For I have no delight in the death of one dying,' says the Lord YAHWEH, 'So turn and live.'" (Ezekiel 18:31f.)

The first of the Two Great Commandments was added to the Golden Thread some time after the preaching of the ethical prophets (Isaiah, Hosea, Amos and Micah) bore fruit in Josiah's reforms. But it was not until the experience of the people's captivity in Babylon that the need to love one's neighbor really caught on. (Leviticus 19:33f.) Jesus' life and the story interpretations of his actions made clear, as did Hosea, what it means to love one's neighbor.

Somewhere along the line of history, the true nature of YAHWEH'S all-knowingness was made plain in Psalm 139. That and such psalms as 8 and 19 and the insights of the poet who gave us the book of Job transformed forever the perception of the true God.

One must never look to man to see what YAHWEH is like. He must look to YAHWEH to see what man should be like. YAHWEH may not in any way be made in the image of humans. It is by this that it becomes clear that man is made in the image of God. This was presented at least by the time of the writers of the Deuteronomic reformation (Genesis 1:27.) However, it never seems really to be assimilated entirely in the Bible since so many human characteristics are applied to YAHWEH even through the New Testament—the worst of which is in the book of Revelation.

Nevertheless, the Golden Thread persists. It begins with the pagan vision of gods in the image of men, the need for intercessors, the wrathful vs the loving Father, His vengeful, parochial, fear inspiring nature that leads to a frantic searching for excuses for sin and the formal incantations and rituals to placate an angry, finite deity.

One thing that needs to be said here for the people of the Old Testament: you never find them excusing their own sinful behavior or blaming it on any other one or thing.

That too is an important part of the Golden Thread, felt throughout its entire length. It is a continuum with no beginning or end. Coming into sight out of the roots of animism, through the meaninglessness of individuals, to where we discover that each human is a special child of a loving Father-Creator who has made each one for a special purpose. We

## The Golden Thread

are called to make our way to heaven here in our earthly existence and so in the hereafter.

What begins as a belief in a lot of super-human gods, with all the faults of humanity, must be replaced so that all can know the One Creator of all that is, who loves all that He has created; One who is perfectly moral and so perfectly righteous and just, yet with compassion, patience, persistent kindness and love. For He communicates with His creatures constantly revealing His true nature and what is the most blessed life to live on earth and after death of the body.

With all the stages of religious development available to us, it is sad that in very few minds is the progression always steadily upward along the Golden Thread. In no one but Jesus do we find perfection. And yet, he responded to one calling him good teacher: "Why do you call me good? No one is good except One: the God." (Mark 10:18.) He strove to make others see the Father rather than himself.

What is to be found in our minds is a mixture of various stages of maturity. These are the contradictions that we discover are stored away in the attic of our minds. A fellowship of regular methodical study of the Bible and weekly honest discussion will little by little reveal these contradictions to us. Only then can we adequately deal with them.

Argument defined as "little ideas rattling around in bone boxes" can never purge false ideas or opinions or provide Golden new ones. Only true discussion that results from thorough study of the whole Bible can help us deal honestly with the religious misfits to be found lurking in our minds—most of which spring from creeds and dogmas spawned in parochial assemblies. We need to share our insights, and applications of Scripture to daily living and so to sort out the misfits. We can avoid or remove our regressions only by fulfilling the Two Great Commandments as we study and share in our seeking.

The Golden Thread, on which all the precious beads of apprehended revelation of the nature and goodness of YAHWEH and all He created, is to be found at one place or another or in many places in the Bible.

Those who seek it will find it if they seek with all their minds and dare honestly and diligently to share in love with other like seekers. The Father-Creator seeks those who seek Him as He is, for He desires that each of us might love Him and each other as He loves us. As Jesus said:

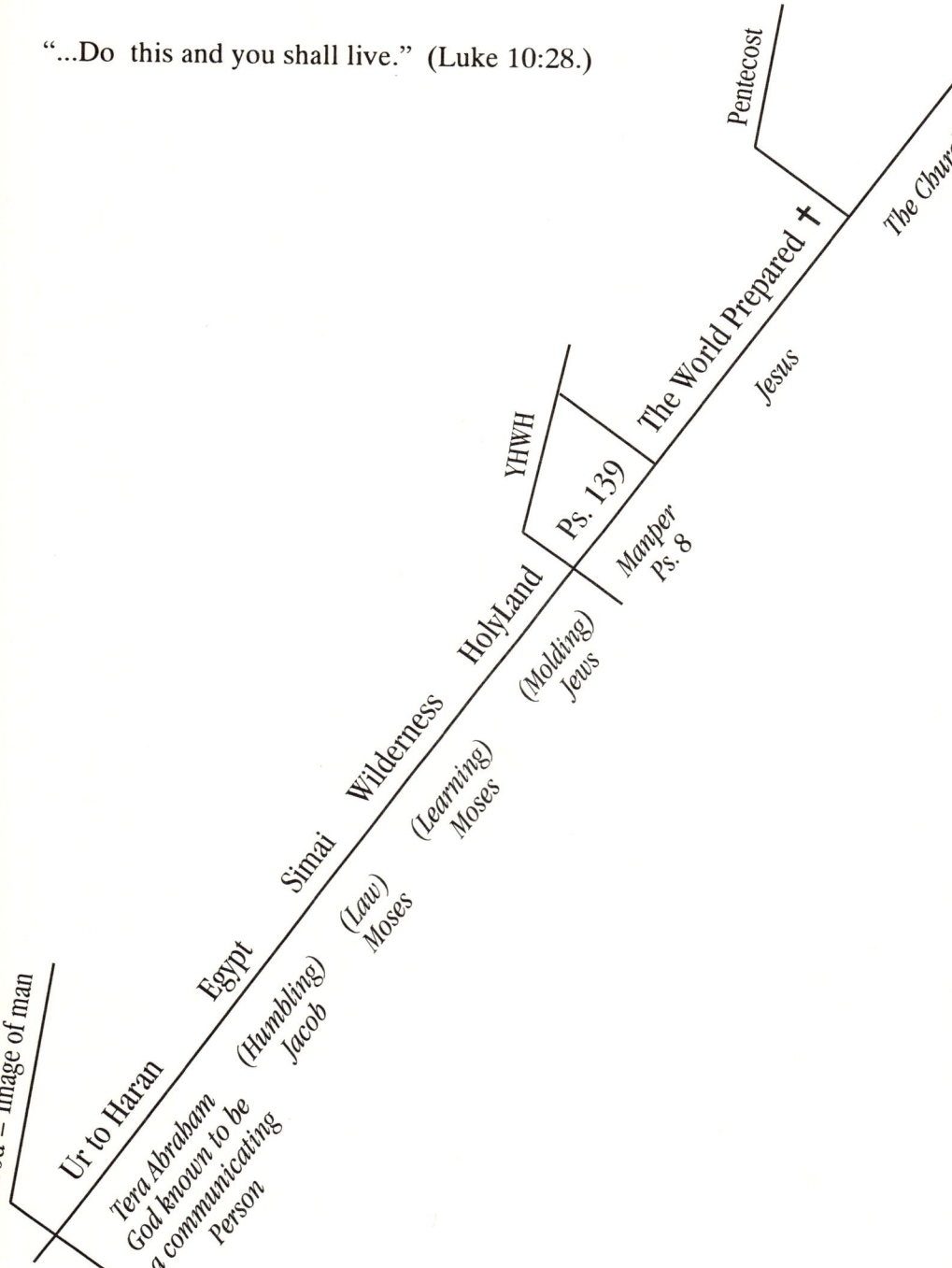

# Chapter 32

# Anything Less Is Idolatry

The Shemag begins: "Listen Israel! YAHWEH is our Strength. YAHWEH is one." What this is saying is that our God is infinite and there is therefore no room for any other. He is one—not many or even three! The evil in having many or even more than one God has been revealed in the undoing of every society that ever held such beliefs.

Look over the great nations of the past and present—Egypt, Babylon, Greece, Rome, Spain, and more recently Germany, France, Britain, Russia, China and, yes, the U.S.A.

The statement in our pledge to the flag, "This nation, under God, indivisible..." is meaningless unless it refers to one and the same God, YAHWEH the infinite, unchanging Father-Creator who is loving, gracious, patient and compassionate.

The only God, alone is worthy of the completely unrestrained love of all His creatures because He is constantly attending to their spiritual needs (not their wants, but their needs.)

As long as the U.S.A. was considered the melting pot where the best that immigrants brought with them was added to the American way of life and the dross cast off, we improved spiritually and prospered. There was the demonstration that the Judaeo-Christian work ethic was keeping wide the door of opportunity to be whatever one wanted to be. We had a common freedom to achieve a common goal under the God who made it all possible. In such an atmosphere it was possible to conceive of ourselves as one family—all children of the same Father-Creator.

"This nation, under God, indivisible..." makes sense if we have the same infinite, loving, YAHWEH in mind, for then we have unity of purpose. I.e., our primary goal is to fulfill the Two Great Commandments in every aspect of personal and social life. All law would then meet the test of these Commandments. How much better the world would be if we were atoned in this fashion.

I know that this is utopian, for as Jesus said: "...for flat and roomy is the way leading to destruction and many are those entering it. But narrow is the gate and difficult the way leading to life and few are those finding it." (Matthew 7:13f.) This was not just a forecast on his part, but an accurate observation of humanity.

Selfishness is the original and perpetual tendency in humans that causes them to strive to make gods in their own image—even reducing the infinite YAHWEH to the physical Jesus of Nazareth—as is done in the visible Church so generally. The various creeds and dogmas of Christendom are full of such forms of idolatry.

Another form of idolatry is seen in the practice of measuring a church by the number of members on the church roll, the size of the budget and how glamorous are its buildings. This gives the wrong picture of the character of YAHWEH. When we see abysmal poverty and ignorance next door to a luxurious cathedral, as can be seen in Ireland, Mexico, Central and South America and even in some of our large cities, we see rank idolatry in action.

However, the Bible itself reveals that many idolatrous beliefs were held by those who gave us this written word. Exodus 33:20 makes YAHWEH physical and yet unapproachable. Genesis 3:11ff., Ecclesiastes 12:13f. and Isaiah 1:18-20 portray Him as a cold, hard judge. Exodus 34:7 and Zephaniah 1:17f. portray Him as vengeful. Exodus 34:14 and Deuteronomy 6:13-15 portray YAHWEH as jealous and one to be greatly feared. The hateful books of Esther, Daniel and especially Revelation, portray Him as the worst of all of these. Such gross contradictions laid alongside of the first of the Two Great Commandments and Exodus 34:6 make it clear that there are a number of contrasting (and mutually

*Anything Less Is Idolatry*

exclusive) versions of the nature of YAHWEH in the Bible.

But it is nevertheless clear to us which of these are the true versions. As it is written in the book of Deuteronomy: "For most near to you is the word, in your mouth and in your mind so you can do it." (30:14.) When we look at the alternatives, there can be no doubt which is the word of YAHWEH.

It does, however, require using all the wisdom and experience the Father has given us, as the prophet Jeremiah recites YAHWEH'S words: "You have sought me and you have found me when you were seeking me with all your mind." (Jeremiah 29:13.) It cannot be done in our spare time or with left over energy. It takes our best, most alert efforts in seeking to know our Father.

To reduce the infinite, all-wise, all-powerful, unchanging, loving, compassionate, patient, gracious, kind and forgiving Spirit Person known to us as YAHWEH to anything less in any way is idolatry. He is what He is. To attempt to reduce Him to any physical being or thing of any sort, or so to represent Him is blasphemous. As Jesus said: "God is spirit and those worshipping Him must worship Him as spirit and truth." (John 4:24.) Anything less is idolatry. It is this that leads me to think that American Indians who worshipped a Great Spirit were more Christian than a lot of members of the visible Church.

When a person puts possessions or money first in his life, he becomes insensitive to the injury he causes to others. Further, he is never satisfied or fulfilled. As the Old Preacher said: "One loving money is not being satisfied by money, nor is the one loving abundance or income." (Ecclesiastes 5:10.) The writer of the First Epistle to Timothy said, "the root of all evil is the love of money..." (I Timothy 6:10.)

When people make power and dominance over other people their god, humans revert to the law of the jungle and behave even worse than animals. Consider all the wars in history and the accompanying atrocities: genocide in the Bible, Buchenwald, the Inquisition, Roman persecution of Christians and Jews and all the heresy trials of Christendom. It is hardly possible to mention all the political oppressions of history. It still prevails in much of our world. Look at Vietnam, Cambodia, China, Iran, Iraq and the Russians in Afghanistan to mention a few.

Another form of idolatry is seen in the plagues brought on by escape techniques resorted to in the 80's. One may include the abuse of drugs (including alcohol and tobacco) where people willingly prostitute their minds to the dominance of such toxic substances at great cost to themselves and to others around them.

Some resort to fantasy or isolation, others to crude and unnatural sex or gluttony. It is true that much of this may be due to loneliness, frustration and other natural human experiences of suffering, but it is all rooted in the consequences of one form or another of idolatry.

Out of fear or just a selfish desire to dominate nature without the care or concern for the desires of the Creator, many evil forces are let loose. Thus we see pollution of soil, water, and air. This also has caused extravagant waste and destruction of natural resources simply because we worship the wrong gods.

When human approval becomes a god, people become slaves to wicked persons. Even if the person whose approval is sought is a kind and wise person, one becomes, more frequently than not, a victim of fallible leadership that is like the blind leading the blind. We have only one God who is always infallible. Even Jesus rebuked one who dared to call him good: "...Why do you call me good? No one is good except one—the God." (Mark 10:18.) There is no other. Anyone less is an idol and unworthy of such trust. But how is one to be sure that he is being led by YAHWEH and not by some false god? My answer is in part 3, chapter 10, Ways YAHWEH Speaks.

Surely, sometimes idolatry creeps up on us. As the writers of Second Isaiah describe it, speaking of a worshipper of idols made of wood: "He does not turn his mind to the facts, there is no knowledge or insight to say, 'One half I burned in the fire, also I baked bread in the coals. I roasted flesh and I am eating. Then the rest I am making an abomination. I am bowing down to a thing of wood!' He feeds on dust, a mind addled, turned aside and unable to deliver himself or to say, 'Is there not a lie in my right hand?'"
(Isaiah 44:18ff.)

There are lots of statues that are not idols. There are lots of idols that are not statues. Our God is that which we let rule our lives. We know that the god(s) we worship determine the way we think and live. So also the way we think and live reveals the god(s) we worship.

*Anything Less Is Idolatry*

How do we choose the clothes we wear, the way we furnish our homes? How do we choose our reading or viewing materials, vote on leadership and issues, choose a vocation and avocations? How do we respond to our neighbor's needs, conduct our stewardship responsibilities from the stewardship of our minds and bodies to national and international matters? All these speak to us of the god(s) we worship.

No one can compel us to worship any particular god(s). We may be led carelessly and blindly to the wrong choice, but that choice is ultimately our own.

What is the true God, YAHWEH, like? How shall we know Him? He is the Father of the prodigal son (Luke 15.) He is like the patient, long-suffering, faithful, compassionate husband of the spouse in Hosea, chapters 1-3. He is the Creator who has made us such exquisite creatures that we are boundless intellectually, entirely free morally, and made never to die but to live—really live—forever. He is YAHWEH God—the holy, just, moral, loving, patient, forgiving, compassionate, Father-Creator who alone fits the first of all rules for a good life in this universe—love. This God alone is truly worthy of our loving worship.

The most remarkable thing about this statement is that no one can prove such a God to you or to me. We can only find Him for ourselves—i.e., we have to do the seeking. When we sincerely seek Him, then we will know what He means when He says: "You have sought me and you have found me when you were seeking me with all your mind." (Jeremiah 29:13.)

It is well worth the effort, for only worship of the one true God brings us peace of mind and living that is not just happy but blessed living. Anything less is idolatry and that is destructive of ourselves, of others and of the world around us.

# PART 10

## PUTTING IT ALL TOGETHER

# Chapter 33

# Mystery

"The hidden things belong to YAHWEH our God but for us and for our children perpetually are the things revealed for doing (lagasoth, lamedh plus Qual Infinitive Construct, no suffix) all this torah." (Deuteronomy 29:29, Hebrew 29:28.) Our Father-Creator has a purpose for all that He has created. He has a purpose for each one of us in His creation. He reveals all that is necessary that we may be able to fulfill that purpose.

There is no need to create mysteries such as is done by religious philosophers and witch doctors or kahunas by whatever name. There are enough genuine mysteries to go around for everyone. Consider some of the most significant: infinity, eternity, spirit, being and not being, curiosity (a God-given hunger of the mind) and the human mind itself.

The Old Preacher said, "...eternity He has given into their minds yet so that humankind (haadham) is not finding what God has done from beginning to end." (Ecclesiasties 3:11.)

We continue to experience new discoveries. Like a snowball rolling down a long hill, the farther it goes, the faster it goes and the faster it goes the faster it accumulates more snow. We see one discovery after another that speeds up the rate of more discoveries. The computer, the "chip", the electron microscope and genetic engineering, that derive from these, are examples. Most all that humans know in the field of science has been discovered in the past two decades.

## Putting It All Together

On the one hand, we feel that modern science appears to be able to uncover all the mysteries of God. On the other hand, when we learn more, we learn how much more there is to know. That is to say, the more we know the more we know we don't know. We are so overwhelmed by what we do not know that, for many, concentration is being directed on the whole of parts instead the of whole of anything.

The farther we get out into space the more elusive becomes any true perception of infinity. We have a hunger for boundaries. We want to comprehend or encircle the universe. But the wider we find it to be the farther away we are from any conception of a boundary. The human mind is boundless in its grasp of limits. Yet it in no way can grasp infinity.

When we are shown that the age of earth and the rest of the solar system is measured in billions of years, we feel we are getting close to some boundaries of time. Then we learn that not only is our solar system young but even our galaxy has older siblings. We see suns that have completed their life span. Then we are off again. We get all kinds of theories or intelligent guesses about how and when the universe began—even about how much longer it will last. That mystery too becomes more of a mystery.

Spirit—intelligent disembodied mind (or self and other consciousness with character) has given rise to a pseudo or semi science we call psychology. But it is as far away from deciphering the relationship between mind and brain as it ever has been.

We know that electric currents reveal that mind is functioning in a brain. There is also a measurable electric current passing between hands touching in love. But that is about as far as science has been able to go. What electric current has to do with thought is as deep a mystery as ever.

The reality of God is mandatory when one lets his mind free to be driven by curiosity. When not shackled by dogmas and creeds, the human mind perceives of its likeness as that of its Creator. It avoids the primitive pit-fall of making a god in human likeness.

Eventually one learns that communication between Spirit and spirit is not at all physical. The person learns that we, being spirit, have a body, that we are not a body. To try to visualize the disembodied spirit leads only to frustration for then we are trying to make spirit concrete or physical.. There is here, then, a feeling of standing on the brink of an abyss.

Still there is the confidence that, although we may know more, we do not expect to know all. As Paul of Tarsus said: "For now we see through a mirror, indistinctly, then (after death of the body) face to face..." (I Corinthians 13:12.) But we must always keep in mind that we are still the creature of the Creator.

What would be if I were not? The solipsist (the ultimate of selfishness) believes that all that is, is in his mind. This would be a fair picture of Hell for it is total conscious isolation—absolute aloneness. Being and not being are not that much of a problem for the one who allows other persons and things to impinge on his consciousness. I am loved and I have objects of my love. I see beauty and pleasing form. I see and experience the effects of both and so am able to judge between them.

I am. I was not. I continue to exist after death of my body. Pursuing the God-given hunger of curiosity has convinced me of this. It shall continue to keep me satisfied eternally and make continued life a challenging, happy adventure. This is so because, as spirit, I am a part of infinity and eternity and I am wrapped snugly in the very midst of the divine mysteries.

"The hidden things belong to YAHWEH our God but for us and for our children perpetually are the things revealed for doing all this torah." (Deuteronomy 29:29.) His mysteries feed my curiosity as hungers of the body and mind are fed in this life on earth by His "things that are revealed."

If we choose, we are dwelling forever in the loving care of Him who is creating and sustaining all that is and is to be. How wonderful and good is our infinite, eternal, all powerful, gracious, patient, kind and compassionate, forgiving and loving YAHWEH Father-Creator. When we know these things we may still be curious about eternity and our future in it but we shall have absolutely no anxiety about it.

# Chapter 34

# Heaven Here and Now

In part 6, chapter 23, Heaven And Hell we noted that no one sends us to hell—or to heaven for that matter. We choose the state in which we shall exist both during this life on earth and after death of the body. To accept fellowship with all the faithful and the presence of YAHWEH is to abide by the Two Great Commandments.

How this works out in daily living is clearly taught by Jesus of Nazareth: "A new commandment I give to you, that you should love (agapate, Present Subjunctive) each other just as I have loved (agapasa, Aorist Indicative Active) you..." (John 13:34.) Note here that the "beloved disciple" uses that peculiar word that focuses on God-like love, a gracious, selfless, total concern for the welfare of others.

More recently and more frequently, psychologists and psychiatrists are formally recognizing the crucial nature of the healing power of this kind of love. Even from a strictly secular point of view, it is seen that getting sufferers to put their minds elsewhere than on themselves does wonders in mitigating pain and reducing considerably the need for pain killers. There is evidence that it even promotes healing.

Note Jesus' example on the Cross. His first words were: "Father, forgive them (i.e., those crucifying him)..." (Luke 23:34.) Next, he thinks of his followers now devastated by the crucifixion of the one they thought would lift the yoke of Rome from their shoulders. He indicates that they will find relief in Psalm 22. It can lift them from their sorrow and disillusionment (in effect, from themselves.) (Mark 15:34.)

His next thought is for the care of his mother now that her eldest son is taken from her. (John 19:26f.) Eventually he becomes conscious of his tortured body: "I thirst!" (John l9:28.) Then he surveys the work of his life on earth and cries out victoriously, "It has been completed!" (tetelestai, John 19:30.) Again his mind turns to the welfare of another—to the repentant malefactor crucified beside him. Jesus comforts the man with the assurance that he will that very day be with Jesus in paradise. (Luke 23:43.)

Even on the cross he is demonstrating what he means in the new commandment. Finally, he freely commits his future apart from the body to the Father-Creator (Luke 23:46.) This is actually a quotation from Psalm 31:5, "Into thy hand I am committing (Hiphil Imperfect, ephqeedh) my spirit. Thou hast ransomed me O YAHWEH, true God (or Power)."

All this being so, we do not have to labor our minds much to see that we ought not be attempting to live only in the future. Under YAHWEH'S plan and provision, the future is to a great degree determined by the present.

The ritual prayer in Matthew 6:9-13, begins well: "...Father of us, the One in the heavens..." Where is heaven? Naturally, where YAHWEH is. Where is YAHWEH? Everywhere but in an unreceptive soul. To be with Him is to be in heaven here and now as well as after death of the body.

When one is down, he is certainly not in heaven. It is easy for a self-centered person to be preoccupied with frustrations (real or invented), pain, slanderous thoughts of others, ego deflations, loss of physical resources, loss of a loved one or a devoted pet. On the other hand, a person whose thoughts lean toward the needs, losses and welfare of others has little time for his own unsolvable problems. As to those problems that can be resolved, the atoned person does what can be done and gets on with living lovingly and gratefully.

Note people surviving a catastrophy-like destruction of a community. One in the depths of hand-wringing depression and despair laments: "We have lost everything. There is nothing left to live for." Another person says, "We still have our lives and are grateful to survive." The first stands around mourning and does little else. The second is busy lending a hand to others and is getting on with his life and such opportunities as may come for reconstruction.

The first is thinking only of himself. The second has evaluated the situation, accepted what can and what cannot be done, gives thanks to God and moves on in life trying to lighten the burden of others. The first is bitter, seeking whom and/or what to blame or condemn. He is experiencing the depth of hell. The second is rejoicing in love and so, knowing the love of the Father-Creator, experiences heaven itself.

Another example is found in the attitude of hired laborers. Those who think of themselves only, "put in" their time anxious for the day to end. They work solely for the money they might earn. They drag along doing just what has to be done and that is all. Their days are long. They miss the joy of making creative suggestions and of the satisfaction of a job well done.

Others have learned the value of Jesus' teaching: "If someone presses you into service for one mile, go with him two." (Matthew 5:41.) If a person burns under forced labor, he lives in bitterness and resentment. If, on the other hand, he says: "I have here an opportunity to show how Jesus loved. I shall make a gift of this service and give forth more than the law (or condition of employment) requires."

What he does is remove the compulsion of the first "mile" and makes it too a gift of love. Such a person is blessed in what he does even as is the hired laborer who expresses his gratitude for employment by giving a little more each day than is required to earn that day's pay.

Happiness is from within a person. It is a good feeling that does not last. Blessedness is a good feeling that lasts. We might call it love for it comes from YAHWEH. Another word for blessedness is heaven. If we do not have heaven here on earth, we are not likely to have it in the future after the death of the body.

When we always think of a half glass of water as half full; when we always face crises or catastrophes with the question, "What good does the Father-Creator plan to make of this?" When we undertake every service with the "second mile" in mind; when we live with an attitude of gratitude; when we love YAHWEH God and each other as Jesus loved, we are blessed—have heaven here and now.

# Chapter 35

# I Believe Because

As Malcom Muggeridge wrote in "Jesus the Man Who Lives" (Harper and Row, Publishers, Inc., NY, NY 1975) "The religion Jesus gave the world was for an experience, not a body of ideas or principles. It is in being lived that it lives." No one can give or teach another person a religion. Each person's religion is based entirely on his experiences of God in his life. The God he worships determines the life he lives and the life he lives reveals the God he worships. No matter what one professes—what he truly believes is only what experience has verified in his living.

As an illustration: no one steps on a bus without asking where it is going unless it always goes where the route number or destination sign indicates. After experience proves that these are reliable, a person can "have faith" in them. Then one really believes in them.

As a personal example: I believe the Creator is a loving person because my eyes see color and form that is pleasant, comforting and uplifting. When I see the stars on a clear, moonless night—so clear and bright as to seem close enough to touch—I feel a warmth and a presence so overwhelming that I know an intimate, magnificent love. This is as much so in my feeling at the sight of an infant of any species—animal or human. Everyone knows the warm delight of a lovely sunrise or sunset when the sky displays all the illuminated colors that an eye can experience.

From the standpoint of common sense, we know that humans could very well survive without the ability to perceive color. This ability obviously is grace, a gift, a little spicing of life. It is as though the Creator were saying, "I know you do not need these experiences. I just wish to make your life better." To put it another way: "I love you—every human soul." That is why I believe that the Creator loves me and you and everyone else. I have had blind people give me their reasons based upon their senses other than sight. But this is only one of the reasons I believe it. I know it from experiences innumerable both large and small.

The very fact that I exist and that I know that I exist assures me that God cares. There was, is and will be no other one just like me. It is not just that science marvels at the uniqueness of persons, but that I have seen it all my life in many relationships with numerous individuals.

We are enough like each other to be able to get along (if we choose) but equally different in many ways. This is true even of identical twins, those persons who develop from a common egg in the mother's womb. This tells me that my uniqueness was planned by an intellect great enough to create and sustain the universe, yet who is concerned enough about me to make me special.

We know that an intellect great enough to create and sustain our universe is capable of bringing into being such persons as He might choose in any manner. As John the Baptist said it: "God is able of these stones to raise up children..." (Luke 3:8.) But He did not! He chose to enlist His creatures in His work of creation. So the Creator created us as potential parents. Sometimes we fulfill our role by accident, at times in ignorance, and other times with careful planning.

Whether sterile or fertile, married or remaining single, most of us end up as parents. Sometimes we beget or bear our own children. At times we adopt. Other times, we are adopted by children neglected or separated from their biological parents. Very few humans are not parents sometime in their lifetime.

But all of us begin as children. From this relationship we learn many things. We learn about needing someone to love. We learn how much we need to be loved. We learn that we need someone who is special in our life. So we know why the Creator made us like Himself—howbeit a little less of course, because we shall always be the creature and He is the Creator, our parent.

He knows us. We are each one special to Him. He loves and cares for us. I know this to be true because it is a part of my life experience in living. It is not because I have been told of or read the history of humanity in the Bible or elsewhere that I have come to believe. It is only because this history is verified in my own experience or in my presence. That is why I believe.

Then, in the matter of dominion: there is something widely different between humans and all other creatures. It is difficult to think of a gentle cow with large brown eyes standing under a tree, leaning against it with front legs crossed and munching on a straw musing: "I am a cow, but not a good cow. I need to be a better cow. I must work on that."

Of course all humans are not so sensitive to conscience. But those who are make the world so very much better. We know therefore, and can believe, that a good conscience is the Creator speaking. As the prophet records YAHWEH'S words: "...I am putting my law within them, and I am writing it upon their minds..." (Jeremiah 31:33.)

When humans are sensitive to the goodness and sacredness of all creation, they do lovely and constructive things with their dominion. When we love one who loves us, we are very conscientious about how we treat any responsibility the beloved one gives us. So I know that YAHWEH loves us and cares for us constantly. In giving humans dominion, He has made us special among His creatures and has given us special responsibilities. When we return His love, we are very careful about how we fulfill them.

Incidentally, the old covenant of control by fear has never worked to achieve this. Love alone does it. The Book of Revelation likewise fails here. It is the old bad news. Only love (agape and ahabh) can be the evangel—the good news.

One other thing about dominion: that YAHWEH cares directly and intimately is seen in that He has reserved dominion of humans to Himself. The proof of this is seen in what terrible things transpire when any human attempts to dominate another—when any human tries to be God. When we are guided by His rule of love, heaven is known in human relationships. So I have come to know and so to believe.

## Putting It All Together

In regard to life after death of the body: I believe it is good and just according to the life I have lived on earth. I believe it because the Father has been so kind and gracious in all my experiences here. Again and again He has brought forth much good from all the crises or "bad" events in my life. Thus I know that those loving Him never depart or are separated from His love—even after death of the body. I can trust Him to make that life good too.

So it can be seen that our Father-Creator did not just create humankind and then go off to let them propagate and blunder along on their own. He makes known to us in many ways what is best for us. But the most complete of all His revelations is in the written word we call the Bible. I know this from more than fifty years of intimate experience in and with it, most of this in the original languages. It has been most fruitful when I have grown by sharing with others in study of His word. So I believe.

What do you believe and why?
Who is your God and why?

# INDEX

| Reference | Page Number |
|---|---|
| **A** | |
| Acts 2 (Chapter) | 129 |
| Acts 9:3-9 | 138 |
| Acts 11:26 | 130 |
| Amos 5:18ff | 156 |
| Amos 9:2-4 | 78 |
| | |
| **C** | |
| I Chronicles 21:1 | 93 |
| I Corinthians 8:7ff | 86 |
| I Corinthians 12:27 | 130 |
| I Corinthians 13:12 | 173 |
| I Corinthians 14:18 | 52 |
| I Corinthians 15 (Chapter) | 107 |
| I Corinthians 15:3-7 | 138 |
| I Corinthians 15:44 | 69, 138 |
| I Corinthians 15:50 | 138 |
| II Corinthians 1:3f | 50 |
| II Corinthians 11:23-29 | 49 |

## D

| | |
|---|---|
| Daniel 2:47 | 132 |
| Daniel 3:25 | 120 |
| Daniel 4:35 | 159 |
| Daniel 6:26 | 132 |
| Daniel 7:12 | 112 |
| Deuteronomy 4:15ff | 77 |
| Deuteronomy 4:29 | 38, 43, 62 |
| Deuteronomy 6:4 | 67 |
| Deuteronomy 6:4f | 84, 102, 126, 159 |
| Deuteronomy 6:4-9 | 24, 50 |
| Deuteronomy 6:6-9 | 159 |
| Deuteronomy 6:13-15 | 164 |
| Deuteronomy 10:17 | 131, 132 |
| Deuteronomy 12:23 | 100 |
| Deuteronomy 13:1-5 | 101 |
| Deuteronomy 27:6f | 86 |
| Deuteronomy 29:29 | 171, 173 |
| Deuteronomy 30:14 | 165 |
| Deuteronomy 30:19 | 102 |
| Deuteronomy 30:19f | 101 |
| Deuteronomy 30:20 | 102 |
| Deuteronomy 34:5 | 141 |
| Deuteronomy 34:6 | 67 |

## E

| | |
|---|---|
| Ecclesiastes 3:11 | 61, 78, 171 |
| Ecclesiastes 3:19f | 106 |
| Ecclesiastes 5:10 | 165 |
| Ecclesiastes 6:12 | 101 |
| Ecclesiastes 12:13 | 66 |
| Ecclesiastes 12:13f | 164 |
| Exodus 3:14f. | 18 |
| Exodus 3:15 | 24 |
| Exodus 6:3 | 19 |

## Bible Texts Used In This Book

| | |
|---|---|
| Exodus 6:6 | 105 |
| Exodus 9:12ff. | 101 |
| Exodus 14:30 | 106 |
| Exodus 22:29 | 86 |
| Exodus 28:41 | 123 |
| Exodus 33:20 | 164 |
| Exodus 34:6 | 25, 39, 74, 79, 84, 86, 133, 143, 158, 159, 164 |
| Exodus 34:7, 14 | 164 |
| Ezekiel 1:1ff | 38 |
| Ezekiel 18:20 | 95 |
| Ezekiel 18:31f | 160 |
| Ezekiel 21:10 | 120 |
| Ezekiel 37:11 | 100 |

## G

| | |
|---|---|
| Genesis 1 (Chapter) | 61 |
| Genesis 1:2 | 73 |
| Genesis 1:26 | 13 |
| Genesis 1:27 | 13, 62, 65, 160 |
| Genesis 1:27f. | 78 |
| Genesis 1:30 | 100 |
| Genesis 2 (Chapter) | 61 |
| Genesis 2:7 | 78, 100 |
| Genesis 2:19f, 24 | 13 |
| Genesis 3 (Chapter) | 93 |
| Genesis 3:1ff. | 3 |
| Genesis 3:11ff. | 164 |
| Genesis 5:24 | 137 |
| Genesis 6:1-4 | 157 |
| Genesis 6:1f | 119 |
| Genesis 6:3 | 100 |
| Genesis 8:21 | 84 |
| Genesis 11:6 | 7 |
| Genesis 27:5ff. | 14 |
| Genesis 31:13 | 123 |

Genesis 47:25                106
Genesis 48:16                105
Genesis 49:33                141
Genesis Chapter 3            93

# H

Hebrews 2:11                 90
Hebrews 5:7-9                90
Hebrews 5:13f.               24
Hebrews 6:1f.                56
Hebrews 29:28                171
Hosea 1-3 (Chapters)         66, 159, 167
Hosea 1:10                   120
Hosea 10:11                  24
Hosea 11 (Chapter)           66, 101, 159
Hosea 11:1                   120
Hosea 13:13                  120
Hosea 13:14                  105

# I

Isaiah 1:2                   156
Isaiah 1:18-20               164
Isaiah 6:1ff                 38
Isaiah 6:5                   132
Isaiah 12:2                  19
Isaiah 26:4                  19
Isaiah 27:1                  93
Isaiah 29:13                 24
Isaiah 43:6                  120
Isaiah 43:10, 11             158
Isaiah 43:15                 132
Isaiah 44:18ff.              166
Isaiah 45:1ff.               124
Isaiah 45:11                 120

## Bible Texts Used In This Book

# J

| | |
|---|---|
| James 1:13 | 94 |
| James 3:1 | 6, 33 |
| James 4:1f. | 44 |
| Jeremiah 8:5 | 87 |
| Jeremiah 13:23 | 27 |
| Jeremiah 15:10 | 156 |
| Jeremiah 23:7f. | 32 |
| Jeremiah 23:23f. | 19, 49, 74, 78, 69 |
| Jeremiah 24:1ff. | 38 |
| Jeremiah 29:13 | 38, 165, 167 |
| Jeremiah 31:31-34 | 152 |
| Jeremiah 31:33 | 181 |
| Job 1:6 and 2:1 | 119 |
| Job 1 and 2 (Chapters) | 94 |
| Job 2:7 | 94 |
| Job 2:10 | 145 |
| Job 14:7-12, 18ff. | 111 |
| Job 14:7-19 | 100 |
| Job 14:10 | 106 |
| Job 14:13f. | 111 |
| Job 17:1 | 100 |
| Job 19:26f. | 99, 111 |
| Job 21:19, 21 | 112 |
| Job 21:29-31 | 144 |
| Job 21:29-32 | 112 |
| Job 26:13 | 93 |
| Job 32:1 | 144 |
| Job 32:8 | 42 |
| Job 32:8f. | 144 |
| Job 33:12-30 | 45 |
| Job 34:9 | 144 |
| Job 34:14f. | 73 |
| Job 34:31f., 37 | 144 |
| Job 38-31 (Chapters) | 143 |
| Job 38:7 | 120 |

# Index

| | |
|---|---|
| Job 42 (Chapter) | 145 |
| Job 42:1-6 | 144 |
| Job 42:10 | 145 |
| John 3:1-12 | 155 |
| John 3:3 | 109 |
| John 4:23 | 125 |
| John 4:24 | 15, 38, 73, 165 |
| John 6:15 | 121 |
| John 6:45, 45 | 152 |
| John 6:48-63 | 151 |
| John 10:10 | 74, 102, 103 |
| John 12 (Chapter) | 150 |
| John 12:10 | 149 |
| John 13:34 | 56, 57, 91, 124, 150, 175 |
| John 14:12 | 90 |
| John 14:23 | 141 |
| John 14:27 | 108 |
| John 15:10f. | 103 |
| John 15:12f. | 150 |
| John 17:1ff. | 47 |
| John 17:21 | 74, 115 |
| John 17:21-23 | 90 |
| John 17:22 | 71 |
| John 18:15 | 149 |
| John 19:26f., 28, 30 | 176 |
| John 20:2-8 | 152 |
| John 20:19f. | 139 |
| John 20:31 | 121 |
| John 21:4ff., 12 | 139 |
| John 21:15-19 | 87 |
| John 21:15ff. | 150 |
| John 21:20, 24 | 148 |
| John 21:23, 24 | 152 |
| I John 4:01 | 41 |
| I John 4:8 | 51, 75 |
| I John 4:12 | 75 |

## Bible Texts Used In This Book

| | |
|---|---|
| I John 4:18 | 108, 113, 150 |
| I John 5:16 | 87 |
| Jonah 1 and 2 (Chapters) | 78 |
| Joshua 6:25 | 106 |
| Joshua 24:15 | 108 |
| Judges 4:4ff. | 14 |
| Judges 4:11, 17 | 9 |
| Judges 6:11 | 9 |
| Judges 11:31ff. | 86 |
| Judges 17:6 | 10 |
| Judges 18:1 | 10 |
| Judges 21:25 | 10 |

## K

| | |
|---|---|
| Kings 8:22f. | 47 |
| I Kings 16:34 | 86 |
| I Kings 21:5ff. | 14 |
| II Kings 2:11 | 137 |
| II Kings 11:1ff. | 14 |
| II Kings 19:35-37 | 79 |
| II Kings 20:12ff. | 112 |
| II Kings 23.10 | 86 |

## L

| | |
|---|---|
| Leviticus 7:34-36 | 123 |
| Leviticus 16:32-34 | 123 |
| Leviticus 17:14 | 100 |
| Leviticus 19:33f. | 39, 160 |
| Leviticus 19:34 | 84, 126 |
| Luke 1:26ff. | 125 |
| Luke 3:8 | 180 |
| Luke 3:23 | 125 |
| Luke 4:16-29 | 124 |
| Luke 5:4ff | 139 |
| Luke 7:47 | 149 |

| | |
|---|---|
| Luke 9:27 | 128 |
| Luke 9:51-56 | 148 |
| Luke 109, 11 | 129 |
| Luke 10:25-28 | 26, 75, 102 |
| Luke 10:28 | 162 |
| Luke 11:2-4 | 52 |
| Luke 11:20 | 129 |
| Luke 11:24-26 | 27 |
| Luke 12:29f. | 48 |
| Luke 14:15-24 | 107 |
| Luke 15 (Chapter) | 25, 43, 86, 167 |
| Luke 16:13 | 108 |
| Luke 17:20f. | 133 |
| Luke 17:21 | 129 |
| Luke 17:24 | 130 |
| Luke 18:1-7 | 48 |
| Luke 20:27ff. | 140 |
| Luke 22:41 | 47 |
| Luke 22:70 | 121 |
| Luke 23:3, 4 | 121 |
| Luke 23:34 | 175 |
| Luke 23:43 | 70, 90, 176 |
| Luke 23:46 | 176 |
| Luke 24:13-31, 37 | 138 |

## M

| | |
|---|---|
| Mark 1:4 and 9 | 123 |
| Mark 1:9-12 | 124 |
| Mark 3:17 | 148 |
| Mark 5:37 | 148 |
| Mark 6:2f. | 124 |
| Mark 6:16 | 128 |
| Mark 8:27, 28 | 127 |
| Mark 9:1 | 128 |
| Mark 9:2 | 148 |
| Mark 9:2-4 | 137, 138 |

## Bible Texts Used In This Book

| | |
|---|---|
| Mark 9:11, 12, 13 | 127 |
| Mark 9:38-40 | 149 |
| Mark 9:47f. | 114 |
| Mark 10:14 | 57 |
| Mark 10:17 | 91, 152 |
| Mark 10:17ff. | 102 |
| Mark 10:18 | 161, 166 |
| Mark 10:23 | 45 |
| Mark 10:35-40, 41 | 149 |
| Mark 10:41 | 149 |
| Mark 11:14, 20, 22f. | 90 |
| Mark 11:22f | 90 |
| Mark 12:18-27 | 102 |
| Mark 12:18f., 23 | 140 |
| Mark 12:25-27 | 137 |
| Mark 12:30 | 102 |
| Mark: 13:3-27, 30 | 128 |
| Mark 13:32 | 110 |
| Mark 14:32f. | 148 |
| Mark 14:35 | 47 |
| Mark 14:36 | 91 |
| Mark 14:61, 62 | 121 |
| Mark 15:2 | 121 |
| Mark 15:34 | 176 |
| Matthew 1:16, 18f. | 125 |
| Matthew 5:6 | 43 |
| Mathew 5:10 | 129 |
| Matthew 5:41 | 177 |
| Matthew 6:6 | 47 |
| Matthew 6:7 | 51 |
| Matthew 6:9-13 | 52, 176 |
| Mathew 7:13 | 127 |
| Matthew 7:13f. | 164 |
| Matthew 8:12 | 114 |
| Matthew 14:25ff., 28-30 | 90 |
| Matthew 16:21-23 | 126 |

193

| | |
|---|---|
| Mathew 16:28 | 128 |
| Matthew 22:1-14 | 107 |
| Matthew 22:13 | 108 |
| Matthew 22:14 | 107 |
| Matthew 22:23ff. | 140 |
| Matthew 26:39 | 47 |
| Mathew 26:64 | 121 |
| Matthew 27:3f. | 126 |
| Matthew 27:62-64 | 139 |
| Matthew 28:2 | 139 |
| Micah 6:8 | 83 |

## N

| | |
|---|---|
| Numbers 3:12 | 86 |
| Numbers 6:24-27 | 18 |
| Numbers 14:11-20 | 157 |
| Numbers 27:12f. | 141 |
| Numbers 33:38 | 141 |

## P

| | |
|---|---|
| Philippians 4:4, 6f. | 109 |
| Pritchard, James B. | 84 |
| Proverbs 8:23-9:11 | 151 |
| Proverbs 30:8f. | 44 |
| Psalms 2:6f., 6-9 | 120 |
| Psalms 6:4 | 106 |
| Psalm 8 (Chapter) | 38, 160 |
| Psalm 8:3-5 | 158 |
| Psalm 8:3-6 | 63 |
| Psalm 8:5 | 67, 78 |
| Psalm 10:16 | 132 |
| Psalm 19 (Chapter) | 38, 62, 160 |
| Psalm 19:1-4 | 62 |

## Bible Texts Used In This Book

| | |
|---|---|
| Psalm 22 (Chapter) | 25, 50, 176 |
| Psalm 23 (Chapter) | 6 |
| Psalm 24:8, 10 | 132 |
| Psalm 29:1 | 119 |
| Psalm 29:3-9 | 38 |
| Psalm 29:10 | 132 |
| Psalm 31 (Chapter) | 25 |
| Psalm 31:5 | 176 |
| Psalm 34:8 | 25 |
| Psalm 44:22 | 100 |
| Psalm 46:10 | 38 |
| Psalm 49:7f. | 86 |
| Psalm 50 (Chapter) | 51 |
| Psalm 50:12 | 86 |
| Psalm 50:16, 23 | 51 |
| Psalm 50:23 | 91 |
| Psalm 82:1-5, 6 | 120 |
| Psalm 83:18 | 19 |
| Psalm 89:1-10, 19-37 | 119 |
| Psalm 90:10 | 100 |
| Psalm 103 | 101 |
| Psalm 103:10f. | 85 |
| Psalm 104 (Chapter) | 18 |
| Psalm 104:29f. | 73, 79 |
| Psalm 106 (Chapter) | 18 |
| Psalm 111-113 (Chapters) | 18 |
| Psalm 117 (Chapter) | 18 |
| Psalm 130:3f. | 85 |
| Psalm 136:24 | 106 |
| Psalm 139 (Chapter) | 48, 49, 62, 63, 78, 160 |
| Psalm 139:1-2, 4 | 63 |
| Psalm 139:1-3 | 69 |
| Psalm 139:7-10 | 19 |

| | |
|---|---|
| Psalm 139:1-6, 7-10, 13-16 | 78 |
| Psalm 143:2 | 52 |
| Psalm 143:3-7 | 101 |
| Psalm 146:4 | 111 |

## R

| | |
|---|---|
| Revelation 6:9-11 | 90 |
| Revelation 12:7-9 | 94 |
| Revelation 19:16 | 132 |
| Revelation 20 (Chapter) | 90 |
| Romans 8:28 | 25, 49 |

## S

| | |
|---|---|
| I Samuel 8:7 | 37, 129, 131 |
| I Samuel 8:7, 12:12, 19 | 159 |
| I Samuel 8:19f. | 10 |
| I Samuel 9:16 | 123 |
| I Samuel 10:1-10 | 123 |
| I Samuel 10:6 | 78 |
| I Samuel 16:7 | 51 |
| I Samuel 16:13 | 123 |
| I Samuel 28:15, 15 | 137 |
| II Samuel 7:14 | 120 |
| II Samuel 8:2 | 10 |
| II Samuel 14:14 | 100, 111 |
| II Samuel 24:1 | 93 |

## T

| | |
|---|---|
| Thessalonians 5:17 | 47 |
| I Timothy 6:10 | 165 |
| I Timothy 6:15f. | 132 |
| II Timothy 3:15 | 41 |

# Z

Zechariah 3:1-2          94
Zechariah 9:9, 13, 15    126
Zephaniah 1:17f.         164